Faith, Family, and Children
with Special Needs

How Catholic Parents and Their Kids with
Special Needs Can Develop a Richer Spiritual Life

DAVID RIZZO

LOYOLAPRESS.
A JESUIT MINISTRY
Chicago

LOYOLA PRESS.
A JESUIT MINISTRY

3441 N. Ashland Avenue
Chicago, Illinois 60657
(800) 621-1008
www.loyolapress.com

Library of Congress Cataloging-in-Publication Data
Rizzo, David.
  Faith, family, and children with special needs : how Catholic parents and their kids with special needs can develop a richer spiritual life / by David Rizzo.
      p. cm.
  Includes bibliographical references (p.   ).
  ISBN-13: 978-0-8294-3651-8
  ISBN-10: 0-8294-3651-0
1. Families--Religious life. 2. Children with disabilities--Religious life. 3. Spiritual life--Catholic Church. I. Title.
  BX2351.R59 2012
  249.087--dc23
                                                                                2011050924

Faith, Family, and Children
with Special Needs

To my parents, Vincent and Ellen Rizzo, and my in-laws, John and Mary Elizabeth McBride, who have provided me with guidance and insight from above as I wrote this book. May they rest in peace.

To my children Brendan, Colin, Danielle and Shannon who continue to inspire me. You are truly gifts from God.

To my beautiful wife, Mercedes, who has shared this adventure with me.

Contents

Preface

This book grew out of a recognition that my daughter's autism was shaping my own spirituality in a unique way. As I confronted the challenge of raising a nonverbal child, my attempts to connect with Danielle on a spiritual level moved me toward a more visual, associational, and sacramental awareness of the sacred in my life. I began to inhabit a world of mystery and meaning where Danielle's silence and my own became both a sign and bridge to God and the life he wanted me to lead.

I half-heartedly mentioned to my wife, Mercedes, that I wanted to write a book on spirituality for parents of children with special needs. I have lots of crazy ideas and thought no more of it. A week or so passed. Then Mercedes informed me that she had discussed the idea with Loyola Press, which was publishing the *Adaptive Eucharist Preparation Kit* we had developed. They wanted an outline and sample chapter immediately. I've found when things happen that quickly it is good to trust God and begin. So I began.

During the writing process I reached out to other parents of kids with special needs and listened to their stories. I continue to be struck by how similar their experiences were to mine. The fear and embarrassment over disruptive behaviors in church, the longing to provide full participation in the sacraments, the isolation parents can feel, the search for meaning, and the deep spirituality rising out of these struggles made me want to write this book even more.

In addition to this I was able to draw on my own experience of children and adults with disabilities. I am a physical therapist, and this gave me a double perspective—that of parent and professional. I knew from this how important strength and endurance training are to the community of people with disabilities, and how important it is for parents and other caretakers to build spiritual strength and endurance. Last, my understanding of the underlying neural changes in the brains of children with autism and other disabilities gave me an interesting vantage point regarding the learning styles of such children.

Many people helped me with this book and I want to acknowledge all of them. First, of course, are my wife Mercedes and children Brendan, Colin, Danielle, and Shannon. They put up with me during this sometimes difficult process. I can honestly say that there is a good reason authors always acknowledge their loved ones first. Next I wish to acknowledge the families and religious educators who so graciously agreed to share their stories with me: Darlene and Stuart Altschuler, Sherry Boas, Kathleen and Bob Davis, Bernice Engler, Sister Bonnie McMenamin, Maria Rioux, and Grace Thoman. Also, I wish to mention those people who without knowing it contributed through what seemed like ordinary interactions at the time: Beth Barol, Dino Guiliano, Bernard and Jeanette McKenna, Sister Kathleen McPeak, Robert Naseef, and Ronald Rizzo. I want to extend special thanks to Phyllis Hartzell for the great photo and Maureen Whitehurst for her valuable encouragement. Finally, I want to acknowledge everyone at Loyola Press especially Jill Arena, Joellyn Cicciarelli, Steve Connor, Carol Dreps, Joe Durepos, Carrie Freyer, Jim Manney, Tom McGrath, Yvonne Micheletti, Maria Mondragon, and anyone else I may have forgotten to thank.

David Rizzo

1
Meet the God of the Mountain

Parents of children with autism and other disabilities often look to their faith in an effort to deal with what seems like a catastrophic event in their lives. This can lead to a deepening of faith. They discover that being the parent of a special-needs child can lead to a flowering spirituality in the hearts of both parent and child. I know this because it has happened to me. My beautiful twelve-year-old daughter, Danielle, has autism.

The challenges are enormous. Obstacles can seem like mountains when your child is unable to speak or even maintain eye contact for more than a fleeting moment; when he or she flaps hands or shrieks; when your child melts down when routines are broken. In such circumstances parents of children with disabilities struggle to provide their kids with a life of dignity and promise. I know. I know how much this takes. I know how stress can take a huge toll, how parents can feel cut off from the world and even from close family members. Parents of special-needs children can feel cut off from themselves and the lives they once knew.

At such times parents may see the mountains as insurmountable. They may wonder why God has seemingly abandoned them. But there is another way of looking at mountains, an older way. In the Old Testament, mountains are where God dwells. It is no accident that one of the Hebrew names for God is *El Shaddai*, the God of the mountain.

In this book I will explore the spirituality of parents struggling to raise their children in these often chaotic and tumultuous environments. I will provide parents with the information and tools they need to cultivate their own spirituality. This is good for parents and is intimately tied to the development of the child's faith too. The bulk of my faith experiences will be drawn from the deep wellspring of my Catholic Christian tradition. Of course, I invite non-Catholic readers to taste these waters, as well as to tap the spiritual wisdom of their own faith traditions.

Charlie Chaplin has been credited with saying that "life is a tragedy when seen in close-up, but a comedy in long-shot." This is certainly true of the lives of parents of children with special needs. They encounter pressures in their daily lives that parents of typical children cannot imagine. Sometimes you want to tear your hair out. A strong and flexible spirituality can be very helpful at such moments. Parents need to cultivate their own spirit in addition to that of their children. Spirituality lends perspective so that parents can find the much needed comedy in their hectic lives.

People with cognitive disabilities are not spiritually disabled

Many parents of children with special needs sincerely desire to bring their children up in the fullness of the Catholic faith but don't know where to begin. Parents of nonverbal children and those with significant cognitive deficit may not even know that receiving the sacraments or even just getting through Sunday Mass are possible for them. Many are afflicted with a sense of loss, and, indeed, parents of children with severe disabilities must go through a grieving process. This is especially true when parents are still reeling from the shock of diagnosis. Fathers or mothers feel sadness about the loss of many things they had expected to share with their child but now cannot because of the unexpected disability. Parents may fear that faith in God and the sacraments of the church are among those gifts that their child can never have.

This happened to me. When Danielle was three years old, the psychologist at the preschool disabled program informed us about the battery of tests she had given my daughter. All the test results suggested autism. I felt like we had been bushwhacked. Later that day, my wife, Mercedes, asked me why I was so sad.

"I will never be able to walk her down the aisle," I replied, barely able to finish the sentence.

I was lost in all the things I would never be able to share with Danielle. No wedding. No car keys. No grandchildren. I worried that she might never know the joy of receiving her First Holy Communion or even just that God loved her. Thankfully, Mercedes knew better and assured me that no matter what Danielle's disability, God would make himself an important and vital part of her life.

People with cognitive disabilities are *not* spiritually disabled. However, autism and other disabilities definitely affect the way children learn, how they organize information, how they conceptualize and communicate experience, and how they interact with the communities to which they belong. Also, autism (or any disability) affects the spirituality of parents and siblings. It does this because it forces us to confront the spiritual potential of our children on their own terms, not on our own. This confrontation with God changes us.

Some facts about autism and language

Autism is a severe neurological disorder that affects a child's ability to communicate, interact with others, and maintain a normal range of interests. I should point out that autism is a spectrum disorder. There is a wide range of severity from mild to severe both in autistic symptoms and in IQ. As the saying goes, "If you've seen a hundred people with autism, you've seen a hundred people with autism." While they are all unique, they share certain characteristic impairments. These impairments are thought to be the result of changes that occur in the brain shortly after the child is born. The brains of young children with autism tend to be larger than in children without the disorder. Something happens to the way brain cells connect to one another causing a system-wide disruption of neural circuits. This leads to processing problems and loss of function in many areas. These brain changes mostly affect the front of the brain, the part that controls complex tasks such as language and social behavior.

The child has problems learning language and using language in functional ways. This causes many problems, because language is not only important for communication, but is also basic to thinking, forming concepts, relating ideas and events, and creating meaning itself. Henri Delacroix said this well when he wrote "The individual's whole experience is built upon the plan of his language."

Let's think about this a little. Much of our early development is based on learning to attach words to concrete things and events we encounter in the world. We are able to think by internally manipulating these verbal representations and linking them in sentences that express cause and effect, relationships across time and space, and feelings, attitudes, and emotions. Language is key to our ability to understand reality and construct meaning out of life. In fact, this ability is one of the most defining features of human beings. So much so, that the author of the book of Genesis gives language a prominent place in the creation of man and woman.

> So out of the ground the LORD God formed every ani-
> mal of the field and every bird of the air, and brought them
> to the man to see what he would call them; and whatever the
> man called every living creature, that was its name. The man
> gave names to all cattle, and to the birds of the air, and to
> every animal of the field.
>
> —Genesis 2:19–20

Now imagine a world where the parts of the brain that ordinarily allow all this to happen are not working properly. A child with impaired language not only has trouble communicating with others and engaging in typical social relationships, but also has difficulty understanding the world and organizing meaning.

Other ways to understand the world

Fortunately, language is not the only way children learn to accomplish these tasks. Other ways to do these things include nonverbal, intuitive, and experiential abilities based on visual features, images, emotions, and nonlinear associations. Children will ordinarily learn to use both verbal and nonverbal processing to create meaning. Autism makes it harder for children to make full use of verbal processing. However, a large body of research is showing that children with autism often compensate for their language impairments by greater reliance on nonverbal, visual, and associative processing.

A great thinker like Albert Einstein said that his own style of thinking was nonverbal. He said, "The words of language, as they are written or spoken, do not seem to play any role in my mechanism of thought. The physical entities which seem to serve as elements in thought are certain signs and more or less clear images."

It is also interesting that many people believe Einstein may have been on the autism spectrum.

To a large degree the spiritual part of our lives is associated more with this type of nonverbal and emotional processing than with conceptual language. Don't misunderstand me. I'm not saying that spiritually oriented people shouldn't use both processing modes or that one is superior to the other. God gave most of us a brain capable of activating both kinds of brain circuits for a reason. However, many people, even those without disorders like autism, rely more heavily on one than the other. That's what the left brain/right brain distinction is all about. Left-brain processing tends to be more concerned with logic and language, while right-brain processing tends to be more concerned with the intuitive, artistic, and spiritual dimension of life.

A spirituality of relationship and longing

Many of the great contemplative mystics of our Catholic faith tradition exemplify this type of nonverbal, nonconceptual mode of processing. I think immediately of one of my favorites, St. John of the Cross. He describes mystical union with God in his great poem "The Dark Night." Here the great saint and poet uses the language of love poetry to describe how a person wishing to approach God must do so in the darkness of faith.

> . . . I had no light or guide
> But the fire that burned inside my chest.

Conceptualization and sensation have ended. He is in a different realm, guided not by the light of logic but by the longing of the beloved for the Lover, only by "the fire that burned inside [his] chest." For St. John of the Cross this type of darkness is essential to achieving the intense mystical transformation he is writing about. Only when we are in the dark are we ready for our *rendezvous* with the Lover. This is a place where the linguistic faculties cease.

Sight, taste, touch, hearing stopped.

Poetry, song, and art become the only real way to express this experience of mystical union. I don't want to push this point too far. In truth, people with autism and related disabilities tend to be neither mystics nor poets. Nor am I implying that great mystics such as St. John of the Cross had autism or any other disability. Indeed, he was capable of writing very logical and rational prose explaining in clear theological terms what his poems meant. My point is that *people with autism have the visual, imagistic, intuitive, emotional, and associative faculties with which to develop and cultivate a robust spirituality.* They can have a relationship with God and an appreciation of the sacraments, liturgy, devotions, and rituals of the Church. The same is true for the parents of children with disabilities.

The spirituality of people with autism can be described as a spirituality of relationship and longing. With the psalmist, they sing,

> As a deer longs for flowing streams,
>   so my soul longs for you, O God.
> My soul thirsts for God,
>   for the living God.
>
> —Psalm 42:1–2

Spirituality in people with disabilities is a way of organizing experience in non-language-based ways. Parents will *of necessity* tap into their own nonverbal, visual, and intuitive faculties in an effort to better connect with their children and with God.

A spirituality of waiting

My oldest boy, Brendan, is an Eagle Scout. One of the nice things about being the father of an Eagle Scout is that you sometimes get to wake up in camp on a chilly autumn morning and think about life. This particular morning I noticed there were still some wisps of smoke rising skyward from the remains of the camp-fire. Somewhere deep in the cold ash there must have been a hot ember. I couldn't see it, only the bluish gray trail it left in the sky. I thought that the spirituality of parents of children with special needs seemed like that ember—in a sort of suspended state between fire and ice, waiting for God's breath to blow like a giant wind and set it ablaze. They are waiting for the breath of God to ignite the ember of spirit deep inside them.

The ancient Hebrews called God's breath his *ruah*, or spirit, the same breath that moved across the faces of the deep at the creation when land and water were separated. As I stared at the campfire, I thought that this same breath is needed here and now. Parents of children with autism, Down syndrome, cerebral palsy, or any other developmental problem truly are waiting for the breath of God to ignite the ember of spirit deep inside them. At that moment I knew that the spirituality of special-needs parents is in so many ways a spirituality of waiting.

As I said, this book is an attempt to wrestle with the unique spirituality of being a special-needs parent. I think of the patri-arch Jacob, who wrestled with an angel of God the entire night and got his hip knocked out of joint. Autism or any other serious disability can be like the hard kick of an angel's foot against our unguarded hip. However, Jacob persisted through the night. I imagine he waited for the battle to end, and although victory did come, it left an indelible mark. I get an image of Jacob in later years telling his kids, "I had him in a choke hold, but then his foot came out of nowhere!" But just as Jacob could point directly at his hip and remember how God made him a great father of his people, the parent of a child with a disability can point to his or her own bum hip and reflect on that encounter with God, and wait.

A Family Activity
Visit a Shrine

Autism and other disabilities affect the entire family—the parents and siblings as well as the child with disabilities. It is very important to find ways to cultivate the entire family's spirituality. One way my family and I discovered how to do this was to visit nearby religious shrines.

Many shrines in the United States are within fairly easy reach by car. We live about an hour from a beautiful shrine in honor of St. Padre Pio. Fortunately, Danielle loves to ride in the car, so we visited the shrine frequently. Because St. Padre Pio lived in Italy, I used this opportunity to reflect on my Italian heritage and the importance of the Catholic faith to the Italian people. I told my children about a visit I had made to Italy and the beautiful churches and religious art that seem to be everywhere you go. And, of course, I talked about the great food!

Most shrines have a place to kneel and pray silently, and an opportunity to submit prayer intentions. At the St. Pio shrine, each of us voiced our own petitions. The children sometimes prayed to get a good grade on an upcoming test or for their youth league basketball team to win the next game. But they also almost always included a prayer for their sister Danielle to learn how to talk or to be cured of her autism. We did not suggest this; they did it on their own. Mercedes and I would bring Danielle up and pray similar things for her. Sometimes a person from the shrine would stand with us and pray over Danielle for the gift of speech or some other healing.

There's an old saying that God answers all prayers but sometimes his answer is no. This hopefully leads one to finding the right prayer, the one aligned with God's will. As time went by and it became clear that Danielle was not meant to speak in words, I kept searching for prayers. I remember on one occasion praying for God to make Danielle the person he wanted her to be. This turned out to be the prayer God is answering with a silent yes.

Our visits to the Shrine of St. Padre Pio were a wonderful experience for the whole family. Each of us took away something special from it. For me it was an opportunity to connect with my old faith ancestors from Italy and pass some of this on to my children. It also allowed me an opportunity to come to grips with my daughter's autism more deeply, and to see that the difficulties we encounter in life are not always solved the way we want them to be solved, with a flourish from God's magic wand. I learned something about God from this experience. I learned that God's love for us was not limited by our vision of how things should be. God has a wider vision, a wide-angle lens—Charlie Chaplin's "long-shot."

2
Who Is God?

Having a child with a severe disability can make you question whether you know anything about who God is and what he wants from you. This isn't surprising, and it's hardly limited to the parents of children with disabilities.

It's said that the young Thomas Aquinas, at the age of seven, asked his learned teachers at Monte Cassino, "What is God?" Already you can see the keen philosopher's mind in embryonic form puzzling over the "what" of God. I can imagine his teachers quizzically scratching their tonsured scalps and telling young Thomas not to be so impertinent. Now multiply this difficulty by a factor of ten, and you get a clearer picture of why the parents of special-needs children ask, "What is God?"

There's no easy answer to this question for any of us; God is a great mystery. Even Thomas Aquinas, a great philosopher who spent most of his life trying to understand the nature of God, concluded that systematic theology cannot provide the heart with an answer. In 1273, Thomas had a profound mystical experience of the living God. It was an experience so intense, so direct, and so visceral, that Thomas told his friends, "All that I have written seems like straw to me." He stopped work on the *Summa Theologica* that day and left it unfinished. After this he preferred to write about God in his beautiful songs about the Holy Eucharist.

There is nothing wrong with systematic theology. The *Summa Theologica* is a masterful expression of the Catholic mind. Aquinas is revered as both a saint and a theologian and has been dubbed "the angelic doctor," in large measure due to his theological and philosophical insights. However, the point is that even Thomas recognized that God is felt and experienced from the heart. Next to this, everything else "seems like straw."

It's no surprise that we rely more heavily on nonconceptual and nonverbal means of explaining God when raising a child with special needs. Here are some of the emotional, associative, intuitive, and visual ways of understanding who and what God is and what it means to be one of his children.

God is love

A very straightforward way we can connect with God and teach our special-needs children about him is to remember that God is love.

I like to compare the love of my silent daughter with the love of our silent God. Children with special needs show love in many ways. Danielle sometimes grabs our hands, puts them on the sides of her head, and gestures that we are to gently squeeze her temples. At other times she engages me in a game of tickles. Some children with disabilities can sign or say "I love you." Children with disabilities often understand far more than they can express. I frequently tell Danielle that I love her. She often smiles and then takes my hands to give her a head squeeze. She understands. Danielle cannot speak; she has never said, "I love you." However, Mercedes and I have felt deep love in her silence. In this way she is like God.

As a teenager I had what some faith traditions would call a conversion experience. I eagerly poured over the Bible like a new convert. When I found these words attributed to the apostle John, I felt a lightness in my heart that I had never felt before.

> Beloved, let us love one another, because love is from God; everyone who loves is born of God and knows God. Whoever does not love does not know God, for God is love.
>
> —1 John 4:7–8

I copied the passage and placed it in my wallet. I carried it around for years and would take it out to look at from time to time. Then one day I misplaced the yellowed and tattered strip of paper, but I can recite the passage from memory even today. This special passage was a great blessing for me. I rejoice that the God who *is* love can touch the lives of children with special needs, their parents, and all people who in silent but loving hearts seek to know him.

God is relationship

Another way to understand the sacred mystery is to stress the relational aspect of God. God is a Trinity of Father, Son, and Spirit. The Trinity is a relational concept.

How so? The triune God embodies, at least in part, the familial relationship. We proclaim in the Nicene Creed that "I believe in one God, the Father Almighty. . . . I believe in one Lord Jesus Christ, the Only Begotten Son of God, born of the Father . . . begotten not made" and so forth. The third Person of the Trinity, the Holy Spirit, is described as one "who proceeds from the Father and the Son." It's all about relationship.

How do we make this doctrinal formula more concrete and understandable? Once again let us take a cue from our children. Special-needs children have a very real understanding of their relationship with their own fathers and mothers. We can use this to image God. The strong love between father, mother, and child is a concrete representation of the love between God the Father, God the Son, and God the Holy Spirit. If we as Catholic

Christians can cross ourselves "in the name of the Father and of the Son and of the Holy Spirit," then we can see this same God at the center of our own intimate relationships.

God as peace and calm

Another nonconceptual, nonlinguistic way to understand God is by experiencing him as the ground of peacefulness and calm. Parents of children with disabilities need peace and calm badly. Sometimes we feel like Gregor Samsa, the character in Franz Kafka's *Metamorphosis*, who woke up one morning to find he had been transformed into a giant insect, and it was downhill from there!

Kathleen, whose son Connor was diagnosed at age two with an extremely rare brain condition called hypothalamic hamartoma, told me how she was afraid to go anywhere without her cell phone charged and turned on, just in case someone needed to contact her. There was good reason for this, because Connor suffered as many as eighty seizures a day. The whole family was affected; even Connor's brother Christopher, from the age of five or six, might be called on to run for a portable oxygen canister during his brother's more intense seizures. Families of children with cognitive and behavioral disabilities experience extreme stress too. Children with autism and other special needs are often hypersensitive to sound and other sensory phenomena. Such children may be in a prolonged fight-or-flight response that can spread to parents and siblings. Therefore, finding calm and peace in God can be a wonderful and therapeutic experience.

So how do we do this? We must cultivate a prayer life that calms this fight-or-flight state and brings on deep relaxation and the silence of mind and body, where we can discover and commune with God. In short, we must find a sacred space inside.

God felt as awe

One of the most fruitful ways to experience God is to stand in awe of him as reflected in his creation. Mountaintops are great places to survey what God has made. So are sunsets and large bodies of water. Not long ago Lee Ann Womack sang a song called "I Hope You Dance," which has the memorable line "I hope you still feel small when you stand beside the ocean." Something about such experiences invokes a deep feeling of awe. That something is the living God.

People with disabilities, even severe impairments, have such experiences of awe. Beth Barol, a colleague of mine, tells the story of a man with autism who sometimes would walk with her on the grounds of the facility where he lived. He always walked with his head down and shoulders hunched. Beth suggested that he stand up straight and look up at the sky. He couldn't, and she realized that medications can cause a chronic hunched posture. So she took him by the hands and lifted them over his head to stretch out his tight neck and shoulders so he could see the sky. Suddenly his eyes lit up, and a huge smile came upon his face. This man had never seen the sky before, and now he stood in awe of it! Beth realized he was having a deeply moving spiritual experience looking at the sky and the magnitude of it.

Leonardo da Vinci reportedly said, "Once you have tasted flight, you will forever walk the earth with your eyes turned skyward, for there you have been and there you will always long to return." That seems to me a fitting epitaph to this story and reminds me just how powerful feelings of awe are and how they can invoke a deep experience of God in our hearts.

God is mercy within mercy within mercy

Throughout history great Catholic teachers have found innovative ways to tell us about God. Each has wrestled with the sacred mystery and tried to find the right words, the right images, and the right tone to properly express it. Earlier I told the story of Thomas Aquinas's struggles to understand the great mystery of God. Here is a story about the great early-church theologian St. Augustine.

One day St. Augustine was walking along the beach trying to understand the mystery of the Trinity. He struggled; try as he might, he couldn't understand how God could be three Persons in one God. Then he saw a little boy with a bucket running back and forth between the water's edge and a small hole he had dug in the sand. The boy would fill the bucket and pour the water into the hole. He did it again and again. Augustine asked the boy what he was doing. The boy replied, "I'm trying to put the ocean into this hole here in the sand." Augustine laughed and said, "Boy, that's impossible. You can never empty the ocean and pour it into that hole." Then the boy said, "And neither can you understand God or the Trinity." When Augustine recovered from the shock and turned to the boy again, the boy had vanished.

I think there is great humility and honesty in knowing, like Augustine, that we can't understand God in the realm of linear thinking. Logic and syntax break down. There are limits to pure reason, as Kant pointed out to us. Visual images, metaphor, and associations are surer guides. St. Patrick used a shamrock to show how Father, Son, and Holy Spirit could be three Persons in one God. Teachers in the Eastern Church use the analogy of a candle lighting other candles. Thomas Merton and Richard Rohr are two modern-day Catholic teachers who have helped guide me in my understanding of God. Merton described God as "mercy within mercy within mercy." I hear an echo of Merton in these words of Richard Rohr:

> I don't think the important thing is to be certain about answers nearly as much as being serious about the questions.
>
> When we hold the questions, we meet and reckon with our contradictions, with our own dilemmas, and we invariably arrive at a turning point where we either evade God or meet God.
>
> When we hang on the horns of the dilemma with Christ—between heaven and earth, between the divine and the human realms—it creates liminal space. All transformation takes place when we're somehow in between, inside of liminal space.

Finding peace in the desert

Like many parents of children with disabilities, my life post-autism had become disoriented, discontented, and distorted. I looked at my own prayer life to see if I could find a set of spiritual practices I could rely on.

I was no stranger to prayer. As an undergraduate at Rutgers College I would lose myself in the stacks of books in the school library, learning everything I could about Catholicism, the history of the church, and its great saints. I remember reading the works of St. John of the Cross, Thomas Merton, and others who made my heart burn for the love of God. I thought I had a vocation to the priesthood in a contemplative order such as the Trappists or Discalced Carmelites, but by the time I graduated, it became clear to me that my true calling was to live in the world as a layman.

About five years later I found myself rather unhappy and alone and working in the field of urban revitalization and economic development. I wasn't attending Mass either. Then something important happened. I attended a three-day economic-development conference in Arizona. Being something of a workaholic, I spent each day indoors, immersed in the seminars and workshops, learning about land use, redevelopment districts, and urban development action grants. When the lonely three days were over, I emerged into the fresh air and sunshine. I had an hour to kill before heading to the airport to return home, so I wandered until I found myself in a park near a pond with swans and dazzling sun reflected in the water. In the middle of the pond was a huge rust-red sculpture of a man and horse rising out of the water—very Spanish in style. While I was looking at the idyllic scene, all the tension and unhappiness that had been brewing inside me for five years suddenly lifted. In the airport on a cocktail napkin I wrote:

> Since late nights alone in prayer
> Over a volume of St. John of the Cross
> (Long, long out of print)
> I have not known such a peace.

The experience by the pond brought me back into contact with the wellspring of spirit in my life. I felt the God I hadn't felt in five years! When I returned home exhausted and refreshed, my best friend called and asked me to come with him to dinner at his girlfriend's place. They had someone they wanted me to meet. Reluctantly I agreed. That was the night I met my future wife for the first time.

When we started raising children, Mercedes and I incorporated prayer practices and devotions into our family life. Then the autism bomb struck, and once more I was left wondering, *God, where are you?* This led me to unpack my arsenal of prayer practices. There was the Jesus Prayer, whereby you rest in God while silently repeating *Lord Jesus, have mercy on me.* There was Centering Prayer, where you sit quietly with eyes closed and repeat a sacred word silently with an attitude of falling deeply into oneself and into the arms of God, who is your source and well-spring. There were Insight Meditation and Christian Yoga, both borrowed from the faith traditions of the Far East. These and other prayers helped restore calm and peace to my life at a critical time.

Parents undergoing the stress of raising children with disabilities can try these prayers too. This can help you cultivate your own spiritual life so that you can be strong and fit enough to cultivate your child's spirit.

A Family Activity
Conscious Relaxation

I hate it when somebody tells me, "Just relax!" I would protest angrily, "I am not stressed out!" I was wound up tight, but I didn't know what to do to relax.

I'm not alone. We value busyness and "getting the job done." We equate high stress with being a good citizen, a productive employee, and a dedicated parent. This is so ingrained that most of us have forgotten what relaxation feels like or how to get there. This is especially true when you are trying to cope with the added stress of raising a child with disabilities.

God is hard to find in the midst of stressful, hectic lives. In truth, God comes in the gentle whisper of a mother to her son or the calming sound of cicadas on a languid summer night. A wonderful story in the Bible reminds us how God makes himself known to us in myriad small ways, so quietly that it forces us to listen with all our strength.

> [God] said, "Go out and stand on the mountain before the LORD, for the LORD is about to pass by." Now there was a great wind, so strong that it was splitting mountains and breaking rocks in pieces before the LORD, but the LORD was not in the wind; and after the wind an earthquake, but the LORD was not in the earthquake; and after the earthquake a fire, but the LORD was not in the fire; and after the fire a sound of sheer silence. When Elijah heard it, he wrapped his face in his mantle and went out and stood at the entrance of the cave. Then there came a voice to him that said, "What are you doing here, Elijah?"
>
> —1 Kings 19:11–13

I think all families, but especially those with children with disabilities, should sit down together and read this Bible passage aloud. Talk to one another about the importance of listening with all your heart for the "sound of sheer silence." Unless we buy into the idea that relaxation is important and something worth organizing around, it will be hard for us to devote the time and energy needed to find sacred space, set aside time to practice, and hear the gentle whisper of God in our lives.

How do we consciously relax? I have used a technique quite successfully in a group of adults with multiple disabilities who participate in relaxation training at the developmental center where I work. It involves deep breathing and giving your body clear instructions to tighten and relax muscles, starting at the feet, and slowly and methodically working toward the head.

Children, disabled and otherwise, can participate as long as they are able to sit still and follow verbal instructions or imitate what they see adults doing. Most three-year-olds, regardless of disability, would have difficulty with this, but most eight- to twelve-year-olds can do it. Children and adults with cognitive disabilities might need a helper sitting nearby to redirect focus. Session length would start short and gradually increase as everyone learns how conscious relaxation works.

First, sit in comfortable chairs in a circle in a room with dim lights. A small room is better than a large room, and there should be no TV, no radio. Calm relaxation music can be helpful. The leader asks everyone to sit quietly and listen to the sound of their breathing. It is often helpful at first to exaggerate this to get the point across. When I am the leader, I sometimes add the words "breathing in, hear yourself breathing in . . . breathing out, hear yourself breathing out."

After a minute or so you say "Now we are going to tighten up our feet." Tell everyone to make their feet good and tight. "Tighter, tighter, make your feet really tight. Now relax them." The leader visually models what the group is expected to do.

At this point the leader reminds everyone to turn their attention back to their breathing. Encourage everyone to listen to their breathing for a few breaths.

Next the leader says, "Now we are going to tighten both our legs. Make them tight." The leader lifts both legs straight out in front so that everyone can see and imitate it. "Make your legs really tight . . . tighter . . . tighter still. Now relax them," and the leader drops his or her legs to the floor.

Once again the leader has everyone return their attention to breathing as before with a similar verbal formula.

A minute later the leader says, "We are going to tighten our backs and our bellies. Make your back and belly really tight . . . tighter . . . tighter . . . as tight as you can. Now relax." Exaggerate sudden relaxation and return everyone's attention to their breathing.

After a minute the leader says, "Now we will tighten both our arms," and holds them out rigid in front. "Tighten both your arms. Make them as tight as you can, and *relax!*" Go back to awareness of breathing.

Then the leader says "We are going to make our faces tight." Really hamming it up, the leader shows a contorted face. "Squish up your face. Really make your face tight . . . tighter . . . tighter . . . tighter, and *relax!*" Turn attention back to breathing. As leader I always add "Breathing in, I am relaxing. . . . Breathing out, I am relaxed," and repeat it several times. The leader encourages the group to sit quietly and peacefully and to enjoy this feeling of total relaxation. How long this goes on depends on the age and disability level of group members. Usually the leader can tell when it is time to finish the session and will say, "What a wonderful time we have had relaxing! Now we will slowly open our eyes and come back to our lovely day."

You will be amazed at how good you feel.

3
Our Children Go to Church

Children with disabilities tend to make their presence known. At times they can do this very loudly, which can be disruptive and disturbing to people.

Once, our family was on vacation at a large amusement park in Pennsylvania. Danielle was about four years old, and she used to like to scream out loud in a high-pitched voice. Her occupational therapist called such outbursts "vocal stims." They have the same effect as hearing fingernails scratching a blackboard. Danielle did a lot of vocal stimming during this particular vacation. We were having a great time at the park, and Danielle loved the rides, but the excitement seemed to fuel the vocal stims. Parents and siblings become good at ignoring such behaviors, and they can forget that other people may be listening. We were in the gift shop when Danielle let out a loud vocalization. Then I heard an elderly man say, "Is that the little girl who has been screaming for the last two days?" I was annoyed and said something like "She has autism; what's your excuse?" It wasn't a pleasant encounter. So you can imagine why parents like me might be nervous when it comes to taking our children to church.

Why it's a challenge to bring a special needs child to church

Mass is a social event. It is a shared liturgical experience when we come together with others to experience our common identity as the Body of Christ. This is where we encounter Christ in the Eucharist and in one another. In Matthew's Gospel, Jesus reminds us, "For where two or three are gathered in my name, I am there among them" (18:20).

Mass is a challenge for people with autism because autism causes problems related to the social domain. The disorder disproportionately affects the "social brain"—the brain circuits responsible for social behavior and the processing of social information. Thus, people with autism may have difficulty with the social aspect of the Mass. They have difficulty observing the actions of other people and behaving accordingly. You and I can quickly learn when we should stand, sit, or kneel, when to speak, and when to fold hands in prayer. People with autism have difficulty doing this. It can lead to inappropriate behavior and extreme anxiety.

This causes parents to be hesitant to bring a special-needs child to church. We parents want to respect other parishioners and maintain appropriate reverence for the Mass. Also, we don't want to look like bad parents. My friend Sister Bonnie McMenamin, who developed a program for children with special needs in the Diocese of Camden, New Jersey, says that "most of our families will say they feel uncomfortable, that people are looking at them." Some parents have half-jokingly told her they want to wear buttons saying "I'm a parent of a child with autism" so that parishioners won't think bad parenting is to blame. This perception is changing with improved awareness of autism, but such attitudes still exist.

What's more, keeping a special-needs child well-behaved, focused, and in the pew for the entire Mass can be exhausting. Further, I hated being unable to devote my attention to Mass when I was on "Danielle duty."

Confronted with these dilemmas, parents may say, "Why bring the family to Mass at all? Why should we if our child doesn't understand what is going on, is having meltdowns, and disrupting the sanctity of the Mass? If we no longer leave church prayerful and refreshed, why should we go as a family?" Mercedes and I asked this question. I even suggested we attend Mass separately so one of us could stay home with Danielle.

When I mentioned this to Father Phil, our pastor, he told me emphatically that this was a bad idea. He said that we should come to Mass as a family and not care what other people thought. I felt liberated. So we attended Mass as a family, and Danielle gradually developed a better tolerance for it. Most people were able to overlook Danielle's fidgeting and occasional babbling noises. Once in a while she would let out a good bloodcurdling shriek, and I would sink down low in the pew, hoping people wouldn't be able to see me. Usually we made it through much of the liturgy before Mercedes or I felt obligated to spare the parishioners and take Danielle to the anteroom for the remainder of the service.

How to celebrate Mass with a special needs child

It's important for parents of children with disabilities to remember that they have a right and a duty to carve out sacred space for themselves. Many things change in the aftermath of having a special-needs child; some things do not. First and foremost—God still loves you, and you still have a need for intimacy with the Divine. These words of Saint Augustine are still true: "My heart is restless, and it will not rest till it rests in Thee!"

Okay, so what can you do to keep your sanity during Mass when your whole focus seems to have shifted to damage control and putting out fires? Here are some suggestions.

Position in the pew. For starters, I recommend that the child who is disabled sit in between both parents so he or she can't wander away. Maintain physical contact in the pew, including deep pressure or whatever sensory input tends to calm your child. Keep the immediate environment clear of objects that could be thrown, torn, tapped, or tossed. Keep your youngest nondisabled child next to one of you so that he or she does not feel neglected.

Reinforce appropriate behavior. Should edibles be used? This depends on their effectiveness for the child and on the parents' comfort level. I'm not talking about giving your child a hoagie sandwich that leaves trails of crumbs and olive oil on the kneeler. However, a Tic Tac or other breath mint can be very effective and leaves no mess. And don't neglect simple praise. My wife and I get a lot of mileage out of such phrases as "Very good sitting, Danielle," and "quiet hands." We put such phrases on picture cards to quietly show our daughter and not be disruptive with too much talk.

Establish a routine. Repetition and practice improve your child's ability to behave at Mass. Something as simple as sitting in the same pew each Sunday, following along with a picture missal, and physical contact, reassurance, and judicious prompting can work wonders. Learning happens. Repetition and ritual can work for you here. Children with autism often develop rituals in order to minimize novelty and uncertainty for themselves. It just so happens that our liturgy is built on ritual and repetition. Repeated exposure to the rhythms and patterns of the Mass will lead to familiarity, self-assurance, and increased tolerance for your child. This means that you can pay more attention and better immerse yourself in the prayer, music, devotion, and reverence of our holy and living sacrifice.

Use a picture missal. People with autism often compensate for their deficits by relying more on their visual sense. One way to capitalize on this is to use a missal containing picture icons. The picture missal that Mercedes and I developed and used successfully with Danielle is an example of this. (It's available from Loyola Press.) It's based on the Picture Exchange Communication System (PECS), where the child communicates by selecting laminated picture icons and attaching them with Velcro to a sentence strip. PECS is widely taught in special education classes and home programs.

Our picture missal has two icons per page. The first gives body position, and the second shows most of the major parts of the Mass. A parent helps the child hold the missal on the correct page and uses hand-over-hand prompts to point to each icon. Most of the time the child will move into the correct body position; if not, the parent gently assists the child into standing, sitting, or kneeling. Reinforcements such as hugs or squeezes should be used to strengthen successes. This helps give children with special needs the information they need to participate. It takes practice and persistence, but it is well worth it. Once a child knows what is expected of him or her, Mass becomes a whole lot more fun for the child, the family, and the other parishioners.

Handling a Mass meltdown

Even with all this, at some point in the journey there will probably be a Mass Meltdown. The magnitude of this event can vary, but figure it will be somewhere between Three Mile Island and Chernobyl.

In our case, we were coasting along for about three or four years after Danielle made her First Communion without any problems. She accompanied us to Mass every Sunday and reverently received the Eucharist. She could stay in the pew through the homily before needing a short break, typically to use the restroom and stretch her legs before returning to the pew well in time for communion.

Then one Sunday we forgot to give Danielle breakfast before piling into the minivan and heading off to Mass. During the car ride she kept signing "cheeseburger," but we just smiled and told her we would eat after church. The meltdown began as soon as we entered the pew and set down the kneeler to pray before Mass began. In blitzkrieg fashion Danielle grabbed the hymnbook in front of her and tried to throw it across the room. Fortunately I managed to block it. Then she started to scream and struggle in the pew. People were beginning to notice, and she was getting louder. I was able to move her out of the pew, and Mercedes was able to escort her out of the church. I was stunned. Everything had been going so well.

We valued coming to Mass as a family, but Mercedes and I knew we had to make a temporary retreat. We didn't want the bad behavior to become a habit. For the next month Danielle stayed home on Sundays with one of us while the other attended Mass with the other kids. Whoever stayed with Danielle would go to an earlier or later Mass. We gave Danielle some time off. However, we knew that this was only a temporary retreat. We got her back into regular Mass attendance as soon as was reasonable.

This is important. Children with disabilities face many challenges, and there may be difficult stretches when behaviors are at their worst. Taking time off may be a necessary strategy, but this must never become a permanent solution. You must find a way to bring your child back so the family can attend Mass together. In our case, Danielle's exile lasted one month. We brought her back but took prudent steps to prevent a repeat of the previous meltdown, including making sure she ate a good breakfast before church and moving hymnbooks and other items in the pew out of her reach.

Danielle's behavior after her "exile" turned out to be exemplary. She seemed quite happy to be back and took extra care to follow all the appropriate forms, such as pressing her hands together in prayer. She made certain I could see her attention to detail by pointing her folded prayer hands in my direction and nodding to me as if to say "See, Dad, I really want to be here with my whole family in the presence of God." She nodded and made a vocalization to the priest when he held up the Host and said to her "The body of Christ." She knelt quite a long time in the pew after communion and again made sure I saw her praying hands.

At that point I knew that the Mass, the Eucharist, her family, and God were important to Danielle. She had missed being away and was happy to be back. It was nice to know this.

Creative programs for children (and their families)

Some very good programs have been developed to help children with special needs and their families attend Mass more successfully, prepare for sacraments, and make progress in their overall religious formation.

In the Diocese of Camden, Sister Bonnie has organized a series of Welcome and Inclusion Masses in several parishes. The parishes rotate hosting the special Masses according to an established schedule. These Masses are modified so that children with special needs and their parents can participate more easily. Before Mass begins, the children gather around the baptismal font to welcome parishioners. During the entrance hymn the children and the pastor process up the aisle together. The celebration is shorter and quieter than a typical Mass; only one stanza is sung for each hymn, and there is a strict four-minute time limit on the priest's homily. The children's lectionary is used for the readings, and renewal of baptismal promises is substituted for the Nicene Creed. These modifications make it easier for children with disabilities to follow and understand what is going on during Mass, and minimize distractions and sensory-driven behaviors.

Sacramental preparation is another feature of the program. Recently four people with disabilities, ranging in age from nine to twenty-seven, received their first Holy Communion.

Sister Bonnie says that "parents who thought their children would never receive the sacraments have now been told, 'Your child is a child of God, and with baptism come privileges and rights as a member of the Body of Christ, including Holy Eucharist.' This has been a long time coming, but religious educators are getting the message."

Likewise, Darlene and Stuart Altschuler operate a religious education program for children with disabilities in Moorestown, New Jersey. When her oldest son, David, was diagnosed with autism, Darlene noticed a change in her attitude toward church. "My relationship with God was not affected," she says. "My going to church was affected. I didn't want to go. I was afraid what other people would think."

Darlene and Stuart started a program in their parish. Children receive small group instruction in classes broken down by grade level, with heavy emphasis on visual presentation of material. Group Masses are held five times a year for the children and their families. The program provides excellent experiences for children with autism and other disabilities, many of whom are nonverbal. It soon became so successful that children from other parishes began to attend. Danielle attended this program for a year even though we lived in a nearby town and belonged to a different parish.

Buzz Lightyear and the Ten Commandments

Another excellent program is the Special Disciples Program developed by my friend Grace Thoman in the parish of St. Isaac Jogues where we attend. This program features one-on-one instruction in the child's home. Parents are encouraged to participate, and each child's program is individualized. Grace developed this program because of her experience with one particular child who was having significant problems preparing for first communion in the typical religious-formation classroom.

"This child was very challenging," she says. "He couldn't manage in a class of thirty-five kids. He had a high-functioning form of autism and also ADHD. I thought there must be other kids like him who needed a different approach, so I put together a mission statement for a Special Disciples Ministry and presented it to the parish. The DRE and Father gave me full rein."

Since Grace's program is so individualized, she has to be very creative, depending on the needs of each child. She showed me how she prepared materials about the Ten Commandments using a Buzz Lightyear theme, and how she would break prayers down into simple parts so that the kids could follow them better. She incorporates a lot of visual material into her lessons. I was quite impressed with how she used Pinocchio and Jiminy Cricket to teach morality, with their slogan "Let your conscience be your guide."

Grace is proud of the fact that all the children in the program receive their sacraments. "In one year I had twelve kids in the program. I met with each of them once a week, always at home. When we were through, the kids knew their stuff." Several of the kids were able to transition into a typical religious-education classroom. Grace was instrumental in Danielle's religious instruction, including her successful preparation for the sacraments of reconciliation, Holy Eucharist, and confirmation. We will always be indebted to Grace for her hard work and friendship.

Drifting toward Mount Ararat

Parents of children with severe disabilities can easily become isolated from other people. Often they feel no one understands what they are going through. It's possible to lose any sense that you are part of the culture at large. It really is that isolating.

This "us against the world" mentality can become a self-fulfilling prophecy. You start avoiding family gatherings, children's parties, sporting events, and other public places. Going to church is just *too hard*. You dread having to explain a meltdown; you dislike the curious looks of casual passersby, the raised eyebrows of disdain or pity, and the whispered implications that bad parenting is the cause.

I remember these feelings. I felt very isolated in the months after Danielle was first diagnosed with autism. In those dark days I would imagine that my family was adrift in an ark like Noah's on a vast sea of water, set apart from the rest of humanity. We were no longer in control of our lives. Rather we were at the mercy of capricious seas and wind and currents. Everything we knew had vanished. And yet I would look at Danielle and know that in the midst of this isolation and despair there was an ocean of spirit deep within her and the rest of us that buoyed us up and drove us toward Mount Ararat and rainbows.

A poem I wrote in those days ended on a curiously ambiguous but hopeful note

> . . . but when I have looked at the stars
> At those who wear their hair and beard in ringlets of gold,
> I know that the lake is gone
> Its obelisks submerged,

In its place an expansive sea
That all might reach Ararat.

Fortunately, I am an optimistic person, and so is Mercedes, who never allowed me to forget that God was at the helm. In the days and months that followed, I reconnected to the community both in church and in the secular world. I realized that solitude and feelings of isolation can be valuable opportunities for spiritual growth and deepening of our relationships with God as long as the feelings are temporary and do not go on too long. Soon grasses and flowers began to take root in the postdiluvian silt.

A seed falls to the ground

Part of this new growth occurred one Sunday at Mass. Danielle was going through a difficult period with very challenging behaviors. I was worn out and in need of the spiritual rejuvenation that can come from deep immersion in the liturgy. For me this means concentrating on every word and every action happening in front of me on the altar. It means an almost rigid formal adherence to the position of my hands pressed together in prayer, my back vertical as I kneel, my eyes focused on the Host. I find that this attention to detail opens me to the real presence of Christ in the Eucharist and church.

This particular Sunday was a disaster. Danielle was noisy. She kept squirming and trying to crawl under the pew. Mercedes was busy with our other daughter, Shannon, who was still a baby. I had to try to redirect Danielle from her disruptive behavior, and this meant devoting all my attention to her. After several minutes of deep pressure and reassuring words, Danielle managed to calm down. But I was angry inside. I felt the Mass was blown. I was angry at God for putting Danielle in the way of my spiritual enjoyment.

The priest was reading the Gospel, but I didn't care; *the Mass was blown.* Then I heard the following words:

> Very truly, I tell you, unless a grain of wheat falls into the earth and dies, it remains just a single grain; but if it dies, it bears much fruit.

—John 12:24

Wow! This was God meeting me where I was that moment. These words reminded me that the spiritual journey was not something trivial put there by God for my mere enjoyment. No, it was not light entertainment for a Sunday morning. It was serious business involving life and death. Unless a grain of wheat falls to the ground and dies, it remains what it is. But that is not its destiny. I realized God already sees in the seed an abundant harvest, but that fresh tendrils must first burst through the outer kernel, cracking it in the process. I knew then that the false self I had constructed out of my expectations, thoughts, and desires had put me in opposition to the reality of my life as the father of a little girl with a big disability. This meant that the unreal needed to be supplanted by the real. In scriptural language I needed to die to self so that both Danielle and I could live the type of life God had in store for us. The choice was mine: Either I could rail against the storm or I could view each moment as necessary and holy. This meant being present in each moment and doing what needed to be done. The farmer doesn't neglect newly planted kernels of wheat. He tends and waters them. He works hard and looks forward to an abundant harvest.

Help my unbelief

I wish I could tell you that this is a painless process, but it's not. Yet pain is not always undesirable. It has a purpose. I am a physical therapist, and one of our mantras is "no pain, no gain." Sometimes you have to hurt to achieve something desirable. Pain also tells us when something is wrong. I know a man who has a rare condition called congenital insensitivity to pain. You might think that a life without pain would be wonderful, but without the perception of painful stimuli this man has never learned how to protect his hands and feet. He bangs his hands against door frames and doesn't take stones out of his shoes. He has lost several fingers and toes to amputations because he cannot feel pain.

One of the things that pain teaches us is that we must seek help from others. The church at its best is a good place to go to when seeking such help. Most people would like to help you if they can. They may not know how to help, but then again, they might. You'll never know if you don't join a community and ask.

In Mark's Gospel we find a story of a man seeking help for his disabled son from the disciples of Jesus. Try as they may, they are unable to help. Fortunately, Jesus is not far away. Let us see what happens when Jesus arrives.

> Someone from the crowd answered him, "Teacher, I brought you my son; he has a spirit that makes him unable to speak; and whenever it seizes him, it dashes him down; and he foams and grinds his teeth and becomes rigid; and I asked your disciples to cast it out, but they could not do so."
>
> He answered them, "You faithless generation, how much longer must I be among you? How much longer must I put up with you? Bring him to me." And they brought the boy to him. When the spirit saw him, immediately it convulsed the boy, and he fell on the ground and rolled about,

foaming at the mouth. Jesus asked the father, "How long has this been happening to him?" And he said, "From child-hood. It has often cast him into the fire and into the water, to destroy him; but if you are able to do anything, have pity on us and help us."

Jesus said to him, "If you are able!—All things can be done for the one who believes."

Immediately the father of the child cried out, "I believe; help my unbelief!" When Jesus saw that a crowd came run-ning together, he rebuked the unclean spirit, saying to it, "You spirit that keeps this boy from speaking and hearing, I command you, come out of him, and never enter him again!" After crying out and convulsing him terribly, it came out, and the boy was like a corpse, so that most of them said, "He is dead." But Jesus took him by the hand and lifted him up, and he was able to stand. When he had entered the house, his disciples asked him privately, "Why could we not cast it out?" He said to them, "This kind can come out only through prayer."

—Mark 9:17–29

This is the Bible passage with which I identify most strongly. Like the father in the story, I have a child with severe disabilities. The father acted with courage when he took his son to the dis-ciples, a proto faith community, for help. Today we would say the boy had epilepsy, perhaps due to a developmental disability. In Jesus' day people attributed such conditions to demons and spirits. It took tremendous courage to ask the disciples for help. When Jesus reminded him that "all things can be done for the one who believes," the man retorted, "I believe; help my unbe-lief!" It almost seems as if he is saying to Jesus, "How much more do you think I can give? If it's not enough, then help me out." I think this ferocious courage comes from the man's deep wound-edness. Jesus responds to this courageous appeal. The church, the community of believers with Jesus at the head, is waiting for us in the same fashion today.

Support groups

Support groups in the church are not usually centered on being the parent of a child with disabilities. They tend to be more general in focus, centered on spirituality and prayer. Sometimes they are organized as men's or women's groups.

For many years I have participated in a men's fellowship group at a parish I attended when I was first married, long before I had a child with autism. It has continued to provide me an opportunity to share my heart with spiritually minded men going through experiences of their own. This group reminds me that I am not the only person going through difficulties. One of our members passed away after a long bout with cancer. Another of our fellowship lost his teenage son suddenly and unexpectedly. I stood sadly with the other group members as a pallbearer at the young man's funeral. Our shared faith in God and in one another has gotten us through tragedies such as these. I recommend joining such a group. If your parish does not have a men's or women's fellowship group, then you might want to form one yourself.

I also recommend attending any good support group specifically for parents of children with disabilities. One such group was formed by Kathleen and Bob, whose son Connor was diagnosed with hypothalamic hamartoma, a rare condition that causes frequent seizures. They felt isolated in rural Ohio, so they used the Internet to locate other families with loved ones having the condition. They cofounded a group called Hypothalamic Hamartoma Uncontrolled Gelastic Seizures, or HHUGS for short. Kathleen said the group has been instrumental in helping her family through some very difficult times.

There are support groups for parents of children with autism. Mercedes and I have attended a group associated with the Autism Society of America. We met many wonderful people, attended great parties and events, and learned how others were successfully coping with being special-needs parents. For a while I attended a group for fathers led by Robert Naseef, a psychologist who is the father of a young adult son with autism. Bob has written eloquently about his experiences, and I benefited greatly from his group.

A Family Activity
Attending Mass

Attending Mass together as a family is so important! We should never allow ourselves to become isolated because we have children with disabilities. We may need to enter a sort of temporary hermitage *for a time*, but at some point we need to return to the world.

One of the best ways I know to do this is to go to Mass as a family. Something profound happens when we see our whole family grow spiritually as each member deepens his or her understanding of our central faith practice. The Mass is a portal to grace that should not be bypassed. This is as true for our children with disabilities as it is for us.

We all learn by doing. This is especially true for people with severe disabilities like autism, where practice and repetition become essential. Children need to learn reverent behavior. They learn it because they experience positive outcomes. Going to Mass every Sunday with parents and siblings who help guide and shape appropriate behavior by providing reinforcement is a powerful way to learn.

Get out into the world! This holds for the secular realm too. Mercedes and I have deliberately exposed Danielle to all sorts of community activities and events. This includes her siblings' sporting events. Our son Colin plays basketball, and we take Danielle to games. There's one problem: She hates the loud buzzer that goes off at various points in the game. She would cover her ears and cry loudly, even long after the buzzer had stopped. I started taking her out of the gym to avoid the painful and disturbing effect it had. I resented missing large parts of the game and thought seriously of staying home with Danielle all together.

Then one day after a game a woman I had never met came up to me. She told me that she had an adult son with autism and she wished she had had the courage to take him to his brothers' games when they were younger. They had always resented how they seemed to play second fiddle to her other son. The woman thought she had missed the opportunity to spend time with them too, and her special-needs son never learned how to behave appropriately in public. When she said good-bye and went to tell her grandson what a great game he had played, I knew that I was doing the right thing in taking Danielle to community events. Also, I knew I was not shortchanging my other children. Ultimately, Danielle learned how to attend such events and enjoys our frequent outings even today.

4

Sacraments for Children
with Special Needs

The sacraments are at the heart of Catholic Christianity, including not only our Roman Catholic tradition but also Eastern Orthodox, high Anglican, and Lutheran traditions. Yet many parents of special-needs children wonder whether their child should receive the sacraments at all. They may ask "Does he really *need* the sacraments?" Often this question is gently dropped in the ear of parents by well-meaning family members and friends who reason that since many children who are cognitively disabled are incapable of committing a mortal sin, they don't *need* the sacraments.

This can seem like a powerful argument, because it taps into parents' fears. "What if my child is turned away?" "Will he be able to sit still in a CCD class?" "Will she understand that the bread is Jesus?" No wonder some feel relieved when someone they love and trust tells them, "Relax. Your child is already holy in God's sight; she doesn't need the sacraments."

Mercedes and I heard this from more than one well-meaning family member. Yet we knew that the sacraments are not just a ticket into heaven. Danielle's autism was severe enough that she is incapable of the conscious rejection of God that is mortal sin, but we wanted her to receive the sacraments anyway. The sacraments lie at the very center of our relationships with God and neighbor.

Why the sacraments are important

The sacraments are a visible sign of the invisible God. This gets at something fundamentally important. We are a curious mix of matter and spirit. They cannot be separated without doing violence to our nature as human persons made in the image and likeness of God. Further, God's incarnation in Jesus means that Jesus is our central sacrament. Our God is invisible. We who live in the world of matter need visible, material signs of his presence. The sacraments are these signs.

Bread, wine, water, and chrism are tangible realities. The smell of fresh bread baking is delightful, but preceding it is a lot of physical work by the farmer who harvested the wheat, the laborer who threshed it, and the miller who ground it into flour. To make bread, you must mix flour with water and yeast, work it into dough with your fingers, knead it with your knuckles and the heels of your hands. It's work! Bread is tangible; it's something you can bless and break, something you can raise to heaven saying, "Take this all of you and eat of it. This is my body, which will be given up for you." It is something you can feel as it is laid in your palm, something you reach for with your fingers and raise to your mouth. It is something you savor as you chew and become one with as you swallow.

This tangible experiential understanding of the sacred in our everyday lives is what the sacraments are all about. They connect us to the invisible God. We *need* the sacraments, and so do our children.

Children with autism are well-equipped to experience sacraments. They rely more on posterior and right-brain circuits to compensate for impairment in the anterior and left brain. These circuits tend to involve sensory processing, especially visual feature analysis. They mediate senses such as touch, hearing, and body awareness. They are more imagistic and associational. This sort of sensory, visual, and experiential processing matches the spiritual understanding that comes from participation in the sacraments. The sacraments are one of the best ways to engage such children in religious and spiritual learning. They *need* the sacraments.

The church's sacramental imagination

One of the most interesting tensions in the history of the church has been between iconographer and iconoclast, picture maker and picture destroyer. At times iconoclasts got the upper hand and destroyed priceless images. People with disabilities would surely side with the iconographers. Vivid visual images adorn our churches. Statues, stained-glass windows, and paintings are more than mere decoration. They teach the faith—something especially important in a world where very few people could read.

People with language problems use icons too. They may use pictures instead of words to communicate. The word used to describe these pictures is *icon*. How marvelous! The word itself associates picture language with the rich iconographic tradition of the church. Just as illiterate peoples in traditional societies relied on visual icons to better grasp God and his relationship with humanity, children with developmental impairments rely on picture icons to discover their own spirituality.

The church's sacramental imagination has flourished in many ways at different times in its history. One traditional activity that has seen a recent revival is the May Crowning, in which children process to the statue of Mary and place a crown of flowers on her head. This honors the Blessed Mother as Queen of Heaven. Processions of all sorts were popular at various times. Medieval mystery plays were performed first in the church, with clerics playing the parts, and later on village greens, with actors. Liturgy and theater have always seemed to me to tap into something ancient and authentic in the experience. They hearken back to cave and hearth, where shamans acted out stories of their travels into the other world and back again.

Even clowns were used in theatrical productions during the Middle Ages to capture the imagination and convey important information about the faith. They established rapport with audiences who responded to the physical humor. Also, clowns could step outside of the action and speak directly to the audience. These traditions intersect with the way many in the developmentally disabled community have learned to forge meaning in their lives.

Sacraments are everywhere

The church's sacramental imagination extends to all of life. Life itself can be sacramental. One's ordinary experiences can become visible signs of the sacred, and living in awareness of such signs can enrich our lives not only as Catholic Christians but also as fathers and mothers of children with special needs.

What do I mean exactly? I mean seeing our children, disabilities and all, as signs of the sacred present among us. It begins with a conscious decision to see your son or daughter as "a finger pointing toward the moon" to use a familiar Zen image. It is even more powerful when you choose an obvious feature of your child's disability itself to be this sign.

For Mercedes and me, this meant seeing Danielle's silence, her inability to speak, as a profound sign of God's silence.

Herman Melville once said, "Silence is the only Voice of our God." We come to feel God in our lives precisely in situations when we are brought to silence, devoid of clear and explicit answers. We may go away unsatisfied, holding our hands up to the sky and voicelessly pleading, but silence speaks. It gives us time to feel, and it changes us. When we recognize the silence as

God's voice, we recognize that time will lead to acceptance. Reality will be what it is, whether we wish it to be or not. God's silence gives us time to appreciate that reality, and in silence embrace it.

Seeing life as sacramental means that we see God in the world around us. Nothing is too small or mundane; in fact, the smaller and more mundane, the better! Even one's breath can be sacramental. Let's recall that our word *spirit* comes from the word for *breath* in Latin. When one is *inspired*, one is filled with *spirit*. Breathing consists of *inspirations* and *expirations*. At the end of life, one *expires*, or *breathes out* one's last *breath*. God breathed his spirit (Hebrew = *ruah* = *breath* = *spirit*) into the first man and woman to give them living souls. An awareness of the energy-carrying capacity of breath puts us directly in touch with spirit. This enlivens us.

Here's another example. I love to walk with my daughters, Shannon and Danielle. On nice evenings at twilight we go to the playground in our neighborhood. When it has been rainy, the large detention basin fills with water like a pond, and we often see Canada geese, mallard ducks, and other waterbirds. Every once in a while a great blue heron lands at the water's edge. He will stand on one leg and gracefully bow to drink of the water. Waterbirds are a powerful sign to me because they bridge the worlds of water, land, and sky the way our lives bridge the worlds of matter and spirit, and the way God bridges the heavens and the earth. They remind us that God is both transcendent and immanent, and that the kingdom of God is both already and not yet.

Jesus taught us to make our neighbors sacraments. We are instructed to see our neighbors, especially those whom we ordinarily think of as the *least* of our brothers, as *identical with Jesus himself.*

Then the king will say to those at his right hand,
"Come, you that are blessed by my Father, inherit the kingdom prepared for you from the foundation of the world; for
I was hungry and you gave me food, I was thirsty and you
gave me something to drink, I was a stranger and you welcomed me, I was naked and you gave me clothing, I was
sick and you took care of me, I was in prison and you visited me."

Then the righteous will answer him, "Lord, when was it
that we saw you hungry and gave you food, or thirsty and
gave you something to drink? And when was it that we saw
you a stranger and welcomed you, or naked and gave you
clothing? And when was it that we saw you sick or in prison
and visited you?" And the king will answer them, "Truly I
tell you, just as you did it to one of the least of these who are
members of my family, you did it to me."

—Matthew 25:34–40

What are we waiting for?

For parents of special-needs children, much time is spent waiting.
We wait for the child to be born. We wait for him or her to
meet developmental milestones such as rolling over, sitting up,
and walking. Parents of children with physical disabilities may
wait far longer than other parents for these events to occur. Parents of children with cognitive disabilities wait for their child to
begin to talk, to put two or more words together, even to say "I
love you, Mommy and Daddy." If the disability is severe enough,
these things may never happen. So we wait. The waiting continues as the child grows older. At family gatherings we wait for our
child to notice that it is her cousin's birthday party and that a
woman dressed like a princess is twisting balloons into animals

and other figures. We wait for our child to join the group of children in the living room who are telling the woman, "I want my balloon to be a dog" or "Can you make mine a hockey player?" We wait as our child sits alone, watching videos of twirling toys and classical music for the hundredth time, uninterested in the other children or the balloons.

Later we wait to see if the parish director of religious education will accept our child into the program or say he must prepare in another parish fifteen miles away. We wait to see if she will be ready to receive first communion at seven years old, or eight years old, or eighteen years old. We wait for our lives to return to normal, for the anger and resentment to pass away. We wait to see if God will answer our prayers. The spirituality of special-needs parents is a spirituality of waiting.

While waiting, I have learned that the only moment you have is the present moment and that you will miss it if you don't pay attention to it. Being comfortable in the present moment is one of the most important things you will ever learn as the parent of a special-needs child.

So how does one embrace the present moment and transform waiting into living?

First and foremost, you must pay attention to breathing. Without changing anything about how you breathe, pay attention to your in-breaths and out-breaths, your inspirations and expirations. Simply feel the rising and falling of your diaphragm while breathing naturally. Every time you breathe in, know that you are breathing in. Every time you breathe out, know that you are breathing out. When a thought arises, turn your attention to the thought and maintain bare attention, becoming aware of the thought as it arises, exists, and falls away. Then return attention to your breath.

This exercise is one of the most powerful tools I know to calm the mind and put myself into the present moment. It is part of a Buddhist practice known as Insight Meditation, a highly effective way to simply watch the mind and body without judging or getting wrapped up or involved in the often destructive self-talk that accounts for much of our thinking. Instead of distancing yourself from life by thinking the same program loop of thoughts over and over again, you just watch the thoughts arise, exist, and disappear. Eventually you see that these thoughts are simply a process that has no real substance. Without suppressing or forcing it, you find yourself able to detach from the thoughts as they lose the power they once had over you.

You don't need to set aside any special time or place to pay attention to the present moment. You can practice it while waiting or while engaged in activity. For instance, if you need to clean up a mess your child has made, turn toward awareness of your breathing. As you reach for a towel, feel yourself reaching for it. As you blot the spill with the towel, become aware of the movement your arm makes and whatever sensations arise during it. If the thought arises, *How could this happen to me?* simply turn full attention to the thought, neither rejecting it nor accepting it; rather, just be aware of it and know when it disappears. You will soon rediscover the present moments in life instead of just waiting for them to be over. Once you rediscover the present moment, you can rediscover God there.

Bridges between the visible and the invisible

The sacraments build bridges from the visible world to the invisible world of spirit. We live in a sensual, tangible, and visible realm, but there's also a hidden world of silence and love, where meaning and belonging are found. This is the sacred world where God dwells. Jesus, in his life, death, and resurrection, is the quintessential bridge between these worlds. The sacraments, and the sacramental view of the world, are the means by which we can fully access the abundance to which Jesus calls us.

The image of a bridge spanning the gulf between visible and invisible, sense and meaning, is the haunting metaphor used by Hart Crane in his great collection of poems entitled *The Bridge*. The final stanza of "To Brooklyn Bridge" is a magnificent expression of the sacramental character of our visible world.

> O Sleepless as the river under thee,
> Vaulting the sea, the prairies' dreaming sod,
> Unto us lowliest sometime sweep, descend
> And of the curveship lend a myth to God.

Your special needs child can be a sign to others

I am constantly amazed how my daughter Danielle touches so many lives without saying a word. When Danielle was about eight, my wife and I were struggling with the question of why God would allow Danielle to remain nonverbal. One day I learned that the state developmental center where I work as a physical therapist was looking into the Picture Exchange Communication System (PECS), a way for nonverbal people to communicate using picture icons. The system is widely used by children with autism, and our speech therapists were hoping to use it with adults. We used PECS with Danielle.

I casually mentioned this to my friend Dino, a speech therapist, and before I knew it, we had arranged to have Danielle demonstrate the system to the entire speech department. I was nervous when Mercedes brought Danielle into the physical therapy gym where we were holding the meeting. I was afraid that she might behave poorly and not be able to show the speech therapists how PECS worked. However, she took one look at the parallel bars in the gym and immediately placed some icons on the sentence strip and gave it to me. The pictures made the sentence *I want sensory play.* The icon for sensory play was parallel bars. Danielle had nailed it. The speech therapists, many of whom had doubted PECS would work, started to talk about trying it.

Dino leaned over to Mercedes and said, "Do you see what just happened? Danielle has just taught us how to help many people at this developmental center and maybe even all the centers in the state." Without saying a word, she had become a sign to others. I remembered two sayings of St. Francis of Assisi: "Preach the gospel always; use words if necessary," and "You may be the only gospel your neighbor ever reads." Surely at this time and place Danielle had become a worthy gospel and a worthy sign of God's love.

A Family Activity
Attend Perpetual Adoration of the Eucharist

One of the most beautiful activities our family does together is to sit before the Eucharist. I recommend it to others.

A parish near ours sponsors perpetual adoration of the Eucharist, during which visitors can drop in and pray before Jesus. I remember how my sons Brendan and Colin would walk along the curb in the parking lot with arms out to the side as if they were on a balance beam. I would carry Shannon in a car seat while a very rambunctious Danielle would run away from Mercedes and me. In summer this took place in the shadow of giant yellow sunflowers that grew in a narrow strip at the edge of the pavement. Somehow we always managed to get ourselves together and enter the small chapel in reverent fashion.

Inside, a large consecrated Host was displayed in a monstrance shaped like the Blessed Mother. The most beautiful thing was that the Host was embedded in the sculpture's frame in such a way as to form a curve of Mary's pregnant belly. One couldn't help but associate this poignant icon with the beautiful words of the Hail Mary: "Blessed are you among women and blessed is the fruit of your womb Jesus." Here we would sit silently for several minutes in prayer and adoration. We sat rapt in the sacred mystery and the beauty of the moment. I felt confident in that moment that we were fed by the mystery and the beauty of the experience, each in his or her own way.

5
Living a Sacramental Life

The sacraments and the sacramental imagination are keys to living out the faith in our families, so let's explore some specific sacraments. We'll begin with baptism.

Baptism

Many children with disabilities receive this sacrament long before their disability becomes known. Children with autism do not begin to show signs or symptoms of the disorder until about 18 months of age.

Danielle was six weeks old when she was baptized in the late autumn of 1998. No one had any idea then that she would be incapable of ever saying the name she was to receive at her baptism. We named her Danielle Mary. Danielle is a feminine version of Daniel, the courageous prophet who was thrown into the lions' den and survived because of his faithfulness to God. Her middle name, Mary, honored her recently deceased maternal grandmother and also Mary the Blessed Mother of Jesus. Autism was the farthest thing from our minds when Mercedes and I presented Danielle for baptism.

Yet many parents present their child for baptism fully aware that the child has special needs. These include parents of children with Down syndrome and other medical conditions that can be detected in the womb by amniocentesis and ultrasound. These courageous parents made the conscious decision to bring their children into the world when abortion could have provided a private way out. They listened to and respected our church's teaching that every life is precious in God's eyes, even those with severe disabilities. Such courageous and faithful parents have a right to expect that the church will be there for their children and support them in full sacramental and liturgical participation.

Baptism is a welcoming into the church community. It is a second birth, whereby we descend into the waters to die to sin, and rise out of the water a new creation. We are given a white baptismal garment to wear as a symbol of this cleansing and rebirth. We are committed to Christ ever after. The sacrament is a reminder that what is false and superficial is washed away, while what is true and flows from our source remains forever. The false self, which would define the person by his or her disability and limitations, gives way to the true self, which flows out of God, the source of all being.

Our descent into the water of baptism is a sharing in Christ's death; our coming up out of the water is a sharing in Christ's resurrection. When a child is diagnosed with a serious disability, parents mourn the loss of the child they imagined they would raise. Reflecting on Danielle's baptism many months after her autism diagnosis, I began to see the sacrament as the death of a falsely imaged Danielle and the rebirth of the true Danielle.

About this time our parish moved from a public school building into our newly constructed church, which contained a large stone baptismal font large enough for full immersion. In my imagination I could hear the water lap against the marble sides of the font like the cold ancient water of the world's oceans. I wrote a poem about this font. I hope this stanza captures something of the mystery and beauty of the sacrament:

How many people will be baptized here?
Immersed, then coming up like humpback whales

Breeching. It's not an accident that the world's
Three-quarters water or that crocuses
Push up through melting snow. Invisible
Is the dance of water nymphs inside rain drops.

Penance and Reconciliation

This sacrament can be a stumbling block. The child's disability
may make it impossible for the child to commit a mortal sin, or
perhaps any sin at all. Still, many children with special needs have
sufficient moral sense to understand when they have acted inappropriately and even to have knowingly sinned. An additional
stumbling block is that the child's communication deficits may
make it very difficult to express himself or herself to the confessor
or to make an act of contrition.

The Bishops' *Guidelines for the Celebration of the Sacraments
with Persons with Disabilities* discusses this difficulty. In paragraph
23 we read,

> Even young children and persons with mental disabil-
> ities often are conscious of committing acts that are sinful
> to some degree and may experience a sense of guilt and sor-
> row. As long as the individual is capable of having a sense
> of contrition for having committed sin, even if he or she
> cannot describe the sin precisely in words, the person may
> receive sacramental absolution. Those with profound mental
> disabilities, who cannot experience even minimal contrition,
> may be invited to participate in penitential services with the
> rest of the community to the extent of their ability.

Darlene Altschuler, whom we met in Chapter 3, has considerable
experience preparing the children in her special-needs religious
education program for Reconciliation. In her program the

children learn a modified examination of conscience using picture icons that begin with "I am sorry and want to do better." The child selects things they can do better from a set of icons, including "Put God First," "Pray More," "Be Good at Church," "Listen to Mom and Dad," "Love My Family," "Say Nice Things," "Love My Neighbor," "Love Myself," "Tell the Truth," "Share," "Forgive Others," and "Be more like Jesus."

It's difficult for kids with special needs to understand this sacrament, and Darlene is the first to admit that her approach may be only a partial solution to the problem. She says, "The implication is that the child wants to do these things better than he or she has been doing them up to this point, which suggests contrition. We want to build on this by developing explicit recognition of sins and also progress the examination of conscience to better reflect the moral abilities and challenges of the child as he or she grows older." Of course the wide spectrum of disability necessitates a need to be flexible and creative in explaining penitential concepts. An explicit recognition of sin could be problematic to some children but attainable by others.

Likewise, we struggled with teaching this sacrament to our daughter. In Danielle's case, we were told she did not need to receive the sacrament of reconciliation before receiving first communion because of her cognitive and communication deficits. However, we felt she might benefit by the reconciliation process provided she was properly supported. Danielle entered the reconciliation room for a face-to-face confession, but she was accompanied by Mercedes and me. Our pastor sat across the table as Danielle handed him a picture icon, which simply said, "I'm sorry." He granted absolution and asked that we read the Act of Contrition aloud for her. Afterward, our pastor told us that he had never experienced anything like that before and that he was glad Danielle had received the sacrament the way she did. While on a verbal and conceptual level it is hard to know how much Danielle understood, on an experiential level she was able to feel the warm and forgiving manner with which the priest received and absolved her. She could relate this to the tangible forgiveness she has experienced in our family.

Modifications like these can be made to enable the special-needs child to make a good confession and receive the grace of reconciliation. Parents and pastors have a lot of latitude in the decision about whether this sacrament is appropriate for any given child. One of the factors influencing this decision is the depth of the parents' understanding of the sacrament. Parents know their children best; they should consider what supports or modifications are needed. Then they must talk to the pastor or director of religious education and arrange for it to happen.

The Holy Eucharist

The Eucharist is central to our Catholic Christian faith. It is one of the most ancient practices of the church. The *Didache*, an early Christian text as old as the New Testament, says

> But every Lord's day gather yourselves together, and break bread, and give thanksgiving after having confessed your transgressions, that your sacrifice may be pure. But let no one who is at odds with his fellow come together with you, until they be reconciled, that your sacrifice may not be profaned. For this is that which was spoken by the Lord: "In every place and time offer to me a pure sacrifice; for I am a great King, says the Lord, and my name is wonderful among the nations."

Given the centrality of this sacrament, it should be no surprise that this is usually the most salient aspect of the child's religious formation for parents of children with special needs. It is a big milestone, wrought with a huge emotional investment. Parents have been fighting for their children since first realizing there was something wrong and going through a painful process of diagnosis, loss, grief, and acceptance. It is no wonder that we might get a little combative now and then. We have had to "fight" school districts, and insurance companies, even God himself in our effort to advocate for our children and provide them the foundation for a meaningful and dignified future. We do this so that they may taste the fruits of meaning and dignity, share them with us, and then one day carry these fruits with them after we pass away. This ferocious advocacy is necessary and honorable. However, sometimes we bring this fighting spirit with us before we have met any resistance at all, and it can negatively color our interactions with those who are trying to help us. There is a tightrope between civility and advocacy that can be very challenging to walk.

Parents of children with special needs feel strongly that their children are capable of relating intimately with Jesus Christ in the sacrament of the Holy Eucharist. And we have no stronger advocate than Jesus himself.

> At the time he was betrayed
> and entered willingly into his Passion,
> he took bread and, giving thanks, broke it,
> and gave it to his disciples, saying:
> Take this, all of you, and eat of it,
> for this is my Body,
> which will be given up for you.
> In a similar way, when supper was ended,
> he took the chalice
> and, once more giving thanks,
> he gave it to his disciples, saying:

Take this, all of you, and drink from it,
for this is the chalice of my Blood,
the Blood of the new and eternal covenant,
which will be poured out for you and for many
for the forgiveness of sins.
Do this in memory of me.

—Eucharistic Prayer II

Jesus offers his precious body and blood to *all of us;* at no point does he qualify this by saying "unless you have atypical brain development."

The National Conference of Catholic Bishops agrees.

> It is essential that all forms of the liturgy be completely accessible to persons with disabilities, since these forms are the essence of the spiritual tie that binds the Christian community together. To exclude members of the parish from these celebrations of the life of the Church, even by passive omission, is to deny the reality of that community. Accessibility involves far more than physical alterations to parish buildings. Realistic provision must be made for persons with disabilities to participate fully in the Eucharist and other liturgical celebrations such as the sacraments of reconciliation, confirmation, and anointing of the sick.

The bishops' guidelines dealing with reception of the Eucharist stipulate that "the criterion for reception of holy communion is the same for persons with developmental and mental disabilities as for all persons, namely, that the person be able to distinguish the Body of Christ from ordinary food, even if this recognition is evidenced through manner, gesture, or reverential silence rather than verbally." Further they add that "cases of doubt should be resolved in favor of the right of the baptized person to receive the sacrament."

In practice this boils down to two things: The child must distinguish the Host from ordinary food, and the child must receive it in a reverent manner.

When Danielle was preparing for first communion, it became clear that specialized educational approaches would be needed to teach her to satisfy these requirements. We were fortunate to have a Special Disciples Ministry in our parish, in which a catechist would come to our home for individualized instruction. We made picture-based materials that helped Danielle distinguish the Host from ordinary food and depicted what was expected in terms of proper and reverent behavior. We were likewise fortunate to have a group sacramental preparation program in one of our neighboring parishes. All of these enabled her to succeed.

Even so, Mercedes and I were nervous as cats when the time came for Danielle to receive her first communion. What if she behaved inappropriately? What if she would not swallow the Host? We thought of a hundred what-ifs, with the last being "What if this is her first and last communion?" But all went well. When Danielle returned to the pew to kneel and pray, it was evident that she had received most reverently. Danielle continues to receive communion frequently; each time I am amazed how fully present she seems during the activity. She may not be able to verbalize what is happening, but she knows in her heart. She knows.

A few years after Danielle made first communion, her older brother Brendan was looking for an Eagle Scout project, and he remembered what we had to go through to make learning materials for her. He decided his project would be to make a special-needs resource library at our parish for nonverbal children preparing for the sacraments. Brendan's project was the basis for our *Adaptive First Eucharist Preparation Kit* (Loyola Press, 2012).

Confirmation

At baptism the infant's parents and godparents speak for the child. In the sacrament of confirmation, the baptized person confirms this commitment. The Bishops' *Guidelines for the Celebration of the Sacraments with Persons with Disabilities* specifically encourages that this sacrament be conferred on children with disabilities regardless of whether they have attained the use of reason.

> Persons who because of developmental or mental disabilities may never attain the use of reason are to be encouraged either directly or, if necessary, through their parents or guardian, to receive the sacrament of confirmation at the appropriate time.

The question for those with developmental or mental disabilities is not can they consent but how can they consent within the limits of their ability to consent, what form that consent might take, and what supports might be needed.

Confirmation is also a time when the Holy Spirit comes to the person receiving the sacrament. People with disabilities are as receptive to the Spirit as their nondisabled counterparts. Cognitive disability does not mean spiritual disability.

Danielle's consent to the power of the Holy Spirit at her confirmation was evident to me as I saw her reverence and delight in the proceedings, shaking her head yes during the renewal of baptismal promises, and her gestures of love to her mother in the pew. In fact, the sight of an obviously disabled child celebrating the sacrament of confirmation in a group setting showed that we all share in the same body of Christ and breathe from the same Spirit as we move through our lives.

Matrimony

People with severe cognitive and developmental disabilities usually do not get married and have children of their own. Yet some people with Asperger's syndrome and high functioning autism do marry, and certainly, marriage is a common vocation in the community of men and women with physical disabilities.

The bishops' guidelines address the sacrament of matrimony specifically requiring that the persons must be legally allowed to marry and that diocesan policies be developed only after consultation with experts who understand the unique needs of people with disabilities. The guidelines say this about the issue of matrimonial consent:

> For matrimonial consent to be valid, it is necessary that the contracting parties possess a sufficient use of reason; that they be free of any grave lack of discretion affecting their judgment about the rights and duties to which they are committing themselves; and that they be capable of assuming the essential obligations of the married state (Canon 1095). It is also necessary that the parties understand that marriage is a permanent union and is ordered to the good of the spouses, and the procreation and education of children (Canon 1096). Pastors and other clergy are to decide cases on an individual basis and in light of pastoral judgment based upon consultation with diocesan personnel involved with disability issues, and canonical, medical, and other experts. Medical and canonical opinions should be sought in determining the presence of any impediments to marriage.

Certainly there are individuals with disabilities who can and will receive the sacrament of matrimony. But my reason for including the sacrament here is to reflect on what it means to parents of children with severe disabilities whose children will never marry.

Happily married parents who see their love for one another as a sign of God's love for humanity naturally hope that their children will experience the sacrament of matrimony too. I was profoundly saddened when I realized that Danielle would never marry. There is the expectation, especially when the child is a daughter (and I fully admit to being politically incorrect when I say this), that you are responsible for her until that day when you lay her hand into the hand of another. At that moment you apply the words of John the Baptist to yourself when he said of Jesus,

> He who has the bride is the bridegroom. The friend of
> the bridegroom, who stands and hears him, rejoices greatly
> at the bridegroom's voice. For this reason my joy has been
> fulfilled. He must increase, but I must decrease.
>
> —John 3:29–30

There is a comfort that the fabric of reality is so woven, that as our own youth fades, our children come into maturity and take over from us. This seems even more so when talking about courtship and marriage and the bringing of children into the world. William Butler Yeats may have been thinking something similar when he wrote

> That is no country for old men. The young
> In one another's arms, birds in the trees
> —Those dying generations—at their song.

So when this expected order in the universe is thwarted by a severe disability, it produces a hole in one's heart that can challenge our trust that we understand reality at all. In fact, it forces us to admit that the picture we have painted about God and what he has in store for us could be a cheap forgery. Yet with time we come to the realization that the only authentic canvas is the one at the end of God's brush, and it is a priceless masterpiece. We realize, of course, that people can live fulfilled lives without being married, and this can reflect God's love for us in as powerful a way. We can see this love reflected when we are called to care for our adult children or siblings who are disabled.

A Family Activity
A Trip Down Memory Lane

A great activity for a family is for parents to share pictures and memories of ourselves receiving the sacraments. Children have a hard time believing that their parents were kids once, doing many of the same things they are doing. The sacraments were milestones in our lives, just as they are milestones in the lives of our children.

Do you have a photo of yourself at your first Holy Communion? I do. Recently I picked up the picture carefully and examined it from all sides, fingering the edges gently so as not to further degrade the yellowing image. I stared at the boy in the picture. I was eight years old and wearing a long white communion gown with a broad gold stripe running down the side. I had a crew cut. It was 1969, and my father cut my hair at the kitchen table. Not long afterward, he finally allowed my brothers and me to grow our hair longer.

It's fun also to dust off those old wedding videos and show them to the kids. If you can't find a VCR anymore, then have the cassettes converted into DVDs. The kids will marvel at how thin and well turned out we were on that special day. They will see their mothers and fathers appear glamorous, like movie stars.

This is a great opportunity to bring photos of your parents and grandparents from their weddings and first communions. It can be a very poignant moment, especially if they are deceased. I am still amazed at how beautiful my mother looked at her wedding and how handsome my father was in his tuxedo.

Two of Mercedes's uncles, now deceased, were priests. Her aunt Kathleen, who is still with us, is a Sister of St. Joseph. I have seen wonderful black and white photos of Mercedes's uncles in their clerical garb, and her aunt in an old style pre-Vatican II habit covering everything but her face. There is even a photo of her uncle George adorning the cover of an old Maryknoll Magazine when he was a young missionary in the Philippines. These provide an excellent opportunity for us to discuss the sacrament of holy orders as well as religious life.

Then show your children photos and keepsakes from their own baptism: baptismal gowns, candles, the white garment you wrapped them in when they were screaming their lungs out, and pictures of their godparents. You can light baptismal candles in remembrance and recall their true identities as beloved sons and daughters of God. Engage your children in reminiscences about their first communion and confirmation. You will be glad you did.

6

Cultivating Compassion, Empathy, and Social Responsibility

Why exactly are compassion, empathy, and social responsibility so hard?

A defining characteristic of autism is difficulty relating to others. Of course, social-skill deficits exist in many people who are not otherwise disabled, but the problem is quite pronounced in autism spectrum disorder. Make no mistake: children with autism and other disabilities want and need strong relationships with family, peers, and others in the community. They frequently have trouble with appropriate social behavior, but that doesn't mean they don't want and need friends.

One of the problem areas is the development of compassion and empathy. Christianity places a great deal of importance on recognizing the needs of others, especially those who are suffering. The ability to recognize a need and respond to it is built upon a foundation of compassion and empathy. Unfortunately, the brain mechanisms governing empathy are largely disrupted in children with autism.

This does not mean that these kids are unable to learn compassion, empathy, and social responsibility. Rather, learning such things is more difficult for them, and they may have limited ability to expresses these traits. However, with proper teaching and much practice, all children can get better at empathy. Compassion and empathy are important for a child's spiritual development. As Catholic parents we have a responsibility to make this a high priority in our children's lives.

Teaching compassion and empathy

Webster defines *compassion* as "sympathetic concern for the suffering of another, together with the inclination to give aid or support or to show mercy." *Empathy* is defined as the "identification with and understanding of another's feelings, situation, and motives." In other words, compassion involves understanding another person's plight and wanting to help. Empathy involves understanding another person's feelings and point of view.

The brain anomalies underlying autism impair the child's ability to manifest these qualities. To have compassion, one must be able to recognize that others are suffering, in pain or in some other undesirable state. The ability to do this depends on recognizing that other people are thinking and feeling different things than I am. People with autism have difficulty doing this. Compassion and empathy also depend on being able to observe another person's face, read his or her body language, and understand what that person is *not* saying. In a sense, you must be able to look into another person's eyes and see his or her soul. These abilities emerge out of the activity of brain circuits in the temporal and frontal lobes that are most affected in autism. And this is only half the challenge. Once you recognize that another person is suffering, you must sympathize and respond appropriately. It's difficult for people with autism to do this.

Difficult does not mean impossible. Research has shown how people with autism will compensate for disrupted brain development by using other parts of the brain. Usually they learn to do this by repeated practice. We've seen how communication can be improved by using visual abilities to compensate for impaired language. Compassion and empathy can be improved by practice in a similar way.

Here are some things parents can do to develop compassion in their special-needs children.

Begin with the child's own emotions. How is he or she feeling now? Start with happy or sad. Make exaggerated facial expressions. Put on a great big smile as you say "happy" and a great big frown as you say "sad." Use exaggerated vocal intonation as well. Ask the child to say how he or she feels verbally or with a picture icon. If it is clear to you how your child is feeling—smiling or laughing for example—provide hand-over-hand assistance to teach the appropriate picture response.

Connect feelings to experience. When the child seems to be catching on and providing consistent verbal or picture responses, you can relate happy and sad to situations the child experiences. For example: assuming your child loves the swing set, say, "When I ride on the swings, I feel—what?" Does he say "happy" using spoken words or a picture icon? If so, then reinforce the response. If not, then provide hand-over-hand assistance until the child can do it independently. If the child hates broccoli, ask, "When I eat broccoli, I feel—what?" You get the idea. Do this with a variety of situations so that the child can appropriately answer how he or she feels in each instance.

Introduce the idea that others have feelings too. Present the same scenarios, only this time ask about the child's sibling or some other person. "When (sibling's name) rides on the swings, she feels—what?" Or try something like this: "When I see (sibling's name) crying, he feels—what?" The point is to get the special-needs child to realize that someone else is feeling an emotion that may be different from what he is feeling himself. Even high-functioning people on the autism spectrum can have a hard time understanding this and relating it to how they should treat others.

When trying to teach special-needs children how they should relate to others, we would do well to recall Jesus' words on the matter: "In everything do to others as you would have them do to you; for this is the law and the prophets." (Matthew 7:12). This saying can be an anchor that you return to each time a teachable moment occurs in the natural environment of your child's life. In addition to the Golden Rule there is the Great Commandment: love God and love your neighbor as yourself. Presenting the information in a compressed format like this is helpful to children who have learned to compensate by becoming predominately rule-based in their thinking.

Moses as a model of compassionate response

I love Moses, the great prophet and leader of the Jewish people, especially the way he responded to the needs of his people. I invite you to place yourself in the story.

The infant Moses escaped death when his mother set him adrift in a papyrus basket, saving him from Pharaoh's command that all young Hebrew boys be killed. He was rescued by the Pharaoh's daughter, who had a kind heart and wanted a baby. She adopted him and raised him in the royal household, even though he was the son of a slave. Later, Moses remembered his origins when he saw a Hebrew slave being severely beaten by an Egyptian. This angered Moses so much that he killed the Egyptian overlord and was forced to flee Egypt.

I can relate to this. Before my daughter was diagnosed with autism, I had been living comfortably, like a nobleman in the royal household. After Danielle was diagnosed I felt like Moses. Instead of being a prince, I was in reality a Hebrew slave. Like

Moses, I found myself coming face-to-face with the injustice of it all. When I saw what autism had done to my little girl, I felt an explosive and compassionate anger at the situation. This caused me to fight blindly for a time and rail at the heavens. I felt forced to flee everything I once knew. Like Moses, I wandered until I arrived at Midian.

At Midian, Moses marries Zipporah, the daughter of Jethro. One day when Moses is at the foot of God's mountain, he sees a burning bush and investigates. There he meets God, who tells him that he hears the groans and cries of the Hebrew slaves and will answer their cries by sending Moses to the Pharaoh to plead for them. Moses is afraid but reluctantly agrees.

I can imagine Moses lying awake in his tent at night thinking *What does this mean to me? I have gotten on with my life, and Midian doesn't seem so bad.* I have felt like this too. Like Moses I have thought I could escape the reality of the situation by throwing myself into day-to-day tasks, making sure the flocks are safe and protected from danger, that my wife and kids are well fed and warm at night. At such times Egypt seems really far away. But just as God did not allow Moses to stay trapped in his own private anger and isolation, I found that I could not stay trapped there either. Like Moses I just couldn't escape the haunting reminders of wrongs to be righted, the echoes of distant chains, the lonely and mournful cry the wind makes, and the voice of God telling me to do something about it. This forced me to see beyond myself and my own private suffering and led me to find the strength to look at the suffering of others. Once I looked, I was able to get up and head back to Egypt, which is a fancy way of saying I was able to rouse myself, get out of my funk, and get more involved in Danielle's life. I began to find ways to advocate for children with disabilities.

Parents of children with disabilities feel liberated when they move beyond seeing a child's disability as their own personal tragedy and instead respond with compassion to all children with disabilities. When we do this, we become like Moses, wielding the staff of God in Pharaoh's court. Confronting the suffering of others and responding with compassion is a life-changing experience. It enables us to move from a self-centered focus on our own tragedy toward a broader focus on helping others.

I invite you to reflect upon how being the parent of a child with a disability has increased your own sense of empathy and compassion. What did you say to Pharaoh? Imagine yourself like Moses wielding the staff of God. Are you committed enough to wield it? Can you show up day after day and stand before Pharaoh on behalf of those whom God has put into your care? Of course you can. By fighting injustice, neglect, and indifference to people with disabilities, you are standing up to Pharaoh. By caring for and nurturing your special-needs child, you confront Pharaoh every day. Finally, how did you move beyond your own isolated private pain to recognize the needs of others? What were some of the ways you experienced God helping you to do this?

The dignity of the human person

One of the foundational building blocks of Catholic social teaching is the dignity of the human person. We all deserve to be treated with honor and respect no matter what condition we are in. Even if we are depleted because of illness, accident, age, or infirmity, our status as beloved children of God holds true. We read this in *The Catechism of the Catholic Church*:

> The dignity of the human person is rooted in his creation in the image and likeness of God (article 1); it is fulfilled in his vocation to divine beatitude (article 2). It is

essential to a human being freely to direct himself to this fulfillment (article 3).

What I find so striking is that all persons possess an inherent dignity and worth precisely because we are created in the image and likeness of God. There is something about us that is worthwhile because we resemble God. We can see something godlike in all human beings, including those with disabilities.

Recognizing this dignity in people with disabilities can be a profound and moving experience. Before we can do this, we adults have to get over the wall of superiority we sometimes put up between ourselves and our loved ones who are disabled. Henri Nouwen says this far more eloquently than I when he writes,

> The great paradox of ministry, therefore, is that we minister above all with our weakness, a weakness that invites us to receive from those to whom we go. The more in touch we are with our own need for healing and salvation, the more open we are to receive in gratitude what others have to offer us. The true skill of ministry is to help fearful and often oppressed men and women become aware of their own gifts, by receiving them in gratitude. In a sense, ministry becomes the skill of active dependency: willing to be dependent on what others have to give but often do not realize they have.

It all seems to come so much easier for children than for adults. I am thinking mostly about the brothers and sisters of children with disabilities. The hours of service they have logged, whether it be for confirmation, scouting, school honor societies, Christian service programs, or just because it needed to be done! Their compassion is heartfelt and real. The brothers and sisters of children with disabilities respond by helping out in every conceivable way. These kids deserve praise for all they've done, from charity walks to being a Special Olympics buddy, from watching a brother or sister so Mom or Dad can get dinner on the table to dressing up in a bunny costume at an autism support group Easter party. They accept the inherent dignity of their brothers or sisters and respond accordingly. I think of my youngest, Shannon, who in many ways has assumed the role of Danielle's big sister, even though she is three years her junior. For Shannon this is perfectly normal. Right now I am looking at an assignment she did for school. She had to nominate someone very special to put on a postage stamp and then design what the stamp would look like. Of course, she nominated her sister, Danielle. The stamp she designed shows Danielle riding a bicycle with Shannon in the background cheering her on. Shannon has seen beyond Danielle's disability.

The ability to recognize the inherent dignity of the human person in a brother or sister with a disability may move the child to see beyond a purely private understanding of the faith as well. It may lead a young person to a broader focus on social justice, extending beyond people with disabilities to encompass the poor, homeless, and oppressed. This happened to my teenage son Colin. He was asked by his cousin Maria to be her confirmation sponsor and as part of the process had to write her a letter explaining in his own words what religion means to him. I am very proud of what he wrote.

> In my view, religion is very important. At school there are lots of community service requirements and I believe it is very important to help those less fortunate. This is an example of modeling yourself after Jesus. To be religious is not just sitting around praying all day; it is simply to reflect the teachings of Jesus and to see others as being made in the

image and likeness of God. Treating people with respect goes a long way toward living a life of happiness. . . . This is why religion is important.

Still, the stress of being the brother or sister of a child with a disability can be challenging. We must be careful not to lay too heavy a burden on these kids. They shouldn't have to feel like the weight of the world is on their shoulders.

One of the more positive things to come out of the increased incidence of autism is that many more people are becoming aware of the inherent dignity of all people, including those with disabilities. However, there are still cases of people being rude and insensitive to the feelings of kids with special needs. Kathleen and Bob, whom we met earlier, encountered such ill treatment directed at their son Connor. This did not come from strangers but came instead from the parish choir of all places. Kathleen told me the story.

"Connor was an altar boy, but he really wanted to sing in the choir. A choir member heard him singing in church one day and thought 'He has a nice voice. We could use him.' So [Connor] sang in the children's choir until he aged out of it. After that he started to sing in the adult choir."

At this point Kathleen explained that the transition to the adult choir was a little challenging, but things seemed to be going well enough until the choir started to prepare for a very special concert. A well-known Catholic song writer was going to visit, and the choir was going to sing for him.

Kathleen continued the story but her voice had become tense, and I could tell how upset she was about what happened next.

"Connor was very excited about it. He went to all the practices and also worked on the publicity for the show. He bought his choir concert outfit. Then the choir director called us and said 'Some of the men were talking—can Connor hand out programs and not sing?' When asked why, the choir director was unable to give an answer."

At this point the emotion could be heard in Kathleen's voice. She paused dramatically.

"Connor sang for the love of singing to God. He was so embarrassed. He had already told everyone he would be singing in the concert. This hit us like a ton of bricks. I might expect this would happen somewhere else but not at a church."

"So what did you do?" I asked her.

"I scheduled an appointment with Father. I told him 'Father, I know you don't have any answers. I'm not looking for an answer. I just want to tell you how I feel.' I told Father that Connor would not be back. No one in the choir asked where he was. It even felt funny going to Mass after that. The way they treated him was wrong, so wrong!" After a moment she added, "Connor is more forgiving than I am."

This story is far from unusual, and I had heard similar sentiments expressed by other parents. I knew that such events can leave deep and lasting scars in both parent and child that can be hard to work through. The dignity of the human person cannot be violated without grave consequence.

A Family Activity
Visit a Convent or Nursing Home

The family is a great place to learn compassion, empathy, and social responsibility, and it is never too early to expose your children to this core dimension of our faith. I remember when I was a new physical therapist working at a nursing home. It was autumn, and the nursing home was having a Halloween party. This was just two weeks after Danielle was born. Brendan was five and Colin was three. Mercedes dressed the children in costumes and brought them to the party.

Many of the residents came out to enjoy the party and see the employees' children, who by now had taken over the place. My boys as always were right in the mix. Mercedes held little Danielle, who looked adorable in her bright orange pumpkin costume and made eyes at all the residents.

I got a lot of compliments that day and enjoyed my status as proud father. But more important, my children were learning that every resident there was a person with an inherent dignity, who had value. And then something strange and poignant occurred. One of the women who lived in this nursing home and had significant dementia wanted to hold Danielle. I was nervous. Danielle was just two weeks old and could not even hold up her head. Mercedes was cautious and not ready to give up her newborn, but she was able to bend down with Danielle so the woman could see her clearly right next to her. A smile lit up this woman's frail ancient face as she sat there. Even at just two weeks of age Danielle bore the image and likeness of God, her Creator, and it was clear enough to be recognized.

Another good way kids and adults in the family can learn compassion is to visit a retirement home for religious brothers or sisters. One Easter, Mercedes's aunt Kathleen, who is a Sister of St. Joseph, had suffered a setback to her health and was unable to leave the "Villa" for the usual family dinner with her nieces and nephews. Mercedes organized an outing, and we all drove out to the Villa to enjoy a nice Easter visit. Our children and some of their cousins met many of the other sisters, some of whom were very frail. Yet this was a perfect opportunity for the kids to spread their exuberance, joy, and energy to these kind sisters. In turn, it was an opportunity for the kids to relate to the sisters on a somewhat different level than they were used to doing, and to see the image and likeness of God in them.

While we were there, Aunt Kathleen showed us the beautiful chapel, and I remembered thinking how fortunate we all were to be spending Easter together. Later the children overran the grounds, but each one found the time to come up to their great-aunt Kathleen and tell her about what was going on in their lives. Danielle enjoyed sitting in a wicker rocking chair, and although she could not speak to her in words, smiled and laughed and, if memory serves, gave her a kiss when it was time to leave and return home at the end of a long and special day.

7
Building Strength and Perseverance

Being the parent of a child with autism or any disability can be draining. To fully understand *how* draining, contrast it with the experience of being the parent of a *typical* child.

The baby comes home to a newly decorated nursery. You busy yourself with learning how to change diapers and set up the playpen. At night you fall asleep, but in the middle of your favorite dream, as you are about to sink the winning putt at Augusta National, you wake to the sound of crying. Not your typical run of the mill crying. No, the highly unpleasant, terrible sound of a newborn's cry. Bleary-eyed, you and your spouse try to calm the baby. You try feeding, you try holding, you try walking the floors. Nothing works. After a couple of hours the baby finally falls asleep and so do you. Yet two hours later it's the same thing all over again. When dawn comes, you barely have the energy to dress yourself.

This goes on for about six months. Somehow you get through it. You know the difficulties are temporary and will pass fairly quickly. Before long the baby is sleeping through the night. Pretty soon you're dreaming that you are wearing a green jacket again. You even look forward to having more children. You look back at these tough times with nostalgia.

For parents of children with special needs, however, the tough times never end. Imagine a state of perpetual sleep deprivation. Imagine having to care for your three-year-old the same way you cared for a three-*month*-old. While other young parents you know are soon able to spend some time by themselves and for themselves, you are caught in the surreal world of autism or Down syndrome or cerebral palsy. You are watching your twelve-year-old all the time so that she doesn't drink the cleaning solution you inadvertently left out. When she does, you have to call poison control, where they know you on a first-name basis.

It is tiring! It exhausts you. You wonder if you can stay in it for the long haul. You question if it's even worth it! You are emotionally drained and spiritually spent.

Every father and mother of a child with special needs feels this way at some point. We have all felt lonely and tired. We have all wondered how we would get through it. We have all held our arms up to the heavens like one crucified, silent and seemingly defeated, while our silent God maintains his silence far longer than we had bargained for.

One day I picked up the phone and called my cousin Ron, whose daughter Cassandra had been diagnosed with autism several years earlier. I wanted to tell him that Danielle had the same diagnosis, and I was hoping he could offer me some guidance on what to do next. Ron told me something I will always remember. "Autism is a long, hard path," he said. I wanted him to tell me something else. I wanted him to tell me it wasn't so hard after all. But Ron didn't say that. He told me that autism was a long, hard path.

Ron was right. Autism *is* a hard path. We have no choice but walk this path. To walk it well, we need strength and perseverance.

Building your strength

One of the most important things I do in my job as a physical therapist is to make people stronger. An illness or chronic disability deconditions people; they lose strength and stamina. Physical therapists prescribe exercise to restore what's been lost. The body responds to exercise by building muscle and endurance. People can become emotionally, mentally, and spiritually deconditioned too, especially when they care for a loved one who is sick or suffers a severe disability.

Nietzsche wrote, "That which does not kill us makes us stronger." The path we walk won't kill us; it will make us stronger. The path itself will help us develop strength and endurance. But just as an athlete trains by running, lifting weights, and doing agility drills, parents need a set of practices they can rely on to develop strength and perseverance to see the path to its end.

My coworker Bernice has a unique perspective on how enduring hardship can be a faith-building experience. Not only does her twenty-year-old son Donald have pervasive developmental disorder (PDD), but she herself was born with significant disabilities. She can't hear in one ear and can't see in one eye. She was born with a three pound tumor in the back of her head which a neurosurgeon had to remove. The doctors gave her a fifty-fifty chance of survival.

Bernice told me that her disabilities have helped her to deal with Don's disability. "It has definitely made me stronger," she said. "When something like this happens, you have to come to terms with the grieving process because you have all these hopes and dreams, and want your child to be all he can be. But you deal with what you have. If you look at the child from the right perspective, they are truly a blessing from God."

She credits God with her ability to find the strength she needs. "God is what holds me together. If it wasn't for him, and my belief and faith, I don't know where I would be. I don't know how I would've done it. God is the only answer."

What can we learn from Jesus about strength?

Jesus told the parable of the sower to teach about the kingdom of God. The parable begins with the familiar image of a man sowing seed across the rural countryside. Some seed fell on the edge of the path, where the birds ate it. Some fell on rocky ground, where there was insufficient soil. Only the seed that fell on rich soil produced an abundant harvest. Jesus explains the parable to his disciples. People respond to the word differently depending on their strength and inner resources. Cares and worries threaten the newly sown seed, but when a person has strength, the seed can germinate, grow, and increase a hundredfold. Then Jesus says something rather shocking.

> And he said to them, "Pay attention to what you hear; the measure you give will be the measure you get, and still more will be given you. For to those who have, more will be given; and from those who have nothing, even what they have will be taken away."
>
> —Mark 4:24–25

Jesus is reminding us that without these precious inner resources of strength and depth there will be nothing we can draw upon, nothing to dip our measuring cup into, and consequently nothing to pull out. We will be left defenseless and unable to cope in a healthy way with all that life throws at us. He is reminding us of the need to tend our field. He is reminding us of the necessity of developing strength and perseverance.

So let's take Jesus seriously and consider what we can do to cultivate these essential qualities in our lives. One of the best ways is to develop a strong prayer life. Finding spiritual support underlies much of what follows here. It certainly has been a strong part of my life. I will discuss how to do this in the next chapter, but what are some other ways beyond prayer to build strength?

Learn about your child's disability

One of my favorite sayings is "Knowledge is power!" This is especially true when dealing with your child's disability. Yet when Danielle was first diagnosed with autism, I had no interest in learning what autism was or why people with autism behaved the way they did. All I knew about autism came from the movie *Rain Man*, and the character in the movie was nothing like Danielle. I was reeling from the shock and disbelief; I wasn't ready to learn about autism.

Time passed, and I realized that I had no way to evaluate what others were saying about my daughter's condition. So I started reading everything I could, especially in the research literature. This knowledge helped me become a better advocate for my daughter. It also helped me to endure the madness that was going on every day and not be defeated by it. Learning about your child's disability gives you power. It builds strength, perseverance, and courage.

Attend events sponsored by support groups and foundations

One of the best ways to stay strong is to become involved in a support group for those affected by disabilities. You learn about how other parents are successfully dealing with the sorts of problems you are facing, and you will go to many fun family events that can lift your spirits and give you perspective.

Our support group has great parties at Halloween, Christmas, and Easter that always seem to end with the children having a terrific time on the dance floor. Likewise there are foundations that sponsor events for children with disabilities. We have visited theme parks and even toured the football stadium where the Philadelphia Eagles play.

Perhaps the best day we had at a foundation sponsored event was a surfing party that Danielle attended. The sponsoring entity was actually called the Best Day Foundation. We had to drive an hour to be at the beach by eight in the morning, but it was well worth it. Danielle really loves the ocean and is a good swimmer. As soon as we arrived, she wanted to go in, immediately. She couldn't figure out why two strangers made her wear a life jacket and helmet, or why they put her on a board and carried her into the surf. But when the first wave hit and she rode it all the way up the beach, she broke out into a huge smile and was hooked.

Find a good babysitter

One of the reasons raising a child with a severe disability can be so demoralizing and draining is that it is very difficult for parents to get out by themselves. Who will take care of your child with special needs? Sometimes your parents can help for a night, but for many this is not a feasible solution. Parents and other family members can be unaware of the degree of surveillance and supervision the child with a severe disability needs.

So it is very important to find a good sitter who is knowledgeable about children with special needs, and whom you can trust. Sometimes you can find a sitter who herself is the sibling of a brother or sister with special needs. Aides from school or people who deliver home behavioral services may make good sitters. So do students studying special education and psychology.

Become a coach or mentor

Another great way to develop inner strength is to become a coach or mentor. You can contribute to the development of your child and other children by helping them learn a sport or some other type of skill.

Danielle participates in Special Olympics gymnastics. I never dreamed I would one day be an assistant coach of a girl's gymnastics team. I am 6 feet 4 inches tall, and gymnastics has never really caught on with American men. I had no experience going into it, but I'm doing fine. It's great fun to be part of the whole team. I even look the part of the famous gymnastics coach Bela Karolyi, a big man surrounded by diminutive female athletes. I continue to be struck by how much this program develops the kids physically and socially.

Eat right and exercise

Exercise and proper diet are very important and easy to overlook. As a physical therapist I know firsthand how exercise lifts depressed moods. When we exercise, our bodies release chemicals called endorphins and enkephalins, which help regulate mood. I cannot overstate the positive health effects of regular exercise and proper diet.

Unfortunately, it is as hard for parents to find the time for exercise as it is to get out to the movies on Saturday nights. You and your spouse might alternate, with one parent exercising while the other watches the kids. It may be possible to include some special-needs children in the exercise activity. You might get a tandem bicycle. The two of you pedal the bike together, while the other parent and siblings ride alongside on their own bikes. This way the entire family can build strength and endurance together.

What to do when your own strength isn't enough?

There's much we can do to get stronger, but all parents of special-needs children come to a point where our own strength just isn't enough. I am reminded of the old Westerns I'd watch as a kid; no matter how quick the hero could draw his gun, there'd be someone in the next town or saloon just a split second faster. Raising a child with special needs is like that. At some point we will meet our match.

This forces us to acknowledge that alone, we are limited, but when we are united to God, the source of all being, we are able to overcome adversity. At such times we are lifted up beyond our limitations and are able to trust that, in the words of Max Ehrmann, " the universe is unfolding as it should."

Job came to this realization too. Recall the Old Testament story. Job had lost everything of value in his life: his children, his possessions, and his health. His friends told him these tragedies were God's punishment for some sin he had committed; the only advice his wife could give him was to "curse God and die." Job could not fathom why he was forced to endure such hardship and suffering. The climax of the story is when God taunts him.

> Will you even put me in the wrong?
>> Will you condemn me that you may be justified?
> Have you an arm like God,
>> and can you thunder with a voice like his?
> Deck yourself with majesty and dignity;
>> clothe yourself with glory and splendor.
>
> —Job 40:8–10

God tells Job that as strong as human beings are, there are creatures still stronger, so strong that only God is powerful enough to prevail against them. One of these creatures is a sea monster named Leviathan. Mockingly, God continues,

Can you draw out Leviathan with a fishhook,
    or press down its tongue with a cord?
Can you put a rope in its nose,
    or pierce its jaw with a hook?
Will it make many supplications to you?
    Will it speak soft words to you?
Will it make a covenant with you
    to be taken as your servant forever?
Will you play with it as with a bird,
    or will you put it on leash for your girls?
Will traders bargain over it?
    Will they divide it up among the merchants?
Can you fill its skin with harpoons,
    or its head with fishing spears?
Lay hands on it;
    think of the battle; you will not do it again!

—Job 41:1–8

It would seem prudent then to ally ourselves with God and let him be our champion in the fight against the monsters in our lives.

This point is presented even more dramatically in the story of Thor and the Midgard serpent in Norse mythology. The god Thor, along with the giant Hymir, is fishing for the Midgard serpent, a creature so large that its body encircles the entire earth. Thor baits his hook with a bull's head and casts it into the sea. As soon as the monster takes the bait, the sea explodes in turbulence and froth. We read in Donald MacKenzie's retelling of the story:

> Thor put forth his entire divine strength and he grew in stature as he pulled the line. At length his feet went through the boat's side, as it tilted over, and they reached to the ocean floor. Harder and harder he pulled and unwillingly the serpent, stung with fierce pain, was hauled through the deep, until its monstrous head came in sight.

The battle continues with Thor striking the monster on the head with his hammer, but before he can land the final blow, his companion, Hymir, cuts the line, and the monster escapes beneath the sea.

For me the Norse version of the story with its epic proportions and heroic tone better describes the fierceness and strength needed when we are locked in conflict with such a monster. Even the giant Hymir is not up to the task. Such strength is reserved for gods only. Autism, cerebral palsy, Down syndrome, or any other serious disability forces us to respond with ferocity and strength. Although we give it our all, with every ounce of strength we possess, it is not until we allow God to do battle for us that we have any chance of victory.

Only then can we proceed confidently, knowing that our God is aware of the challenges and hardships we face. God is our Creator and has great plans for us. After all, as he reminds the prophet Jeremiah, "Before I formed you in the womb I knew you, and before you were born I consecrated you; I appointed you a prophet to the nations" (Jeremiah 1:5).

We cannot help but be strengthened when we remember that God himself has formed and consecrated us before we were born!

A Family Activity

Take a Disability-Friendly Vacation

One of the best ways to build strength and renew spirits is to take a relaxing vacation. Taking a child with a serious disability on the wrong type of vacation, however, can leave you feeling as though you need a vacation from your vacation. To avoid this, plan a *disability-friendly vacation.*

What do I mean exactly? That depends greatly on the individual child's likes and dislikes, temperament, sensory needs, and so on. Nevertheless, disability-friendly vacations have some things in common.

First, choose a place where people expect and tolerate children—those with disabilities and those without. Go to a place where children are running up and down, making noise and enjoying themselves. Avoid places where children are scarce, where the ones you do find walk around in knickers and end every sentence with "ma'am" or "sir," and where careless steps could result in breaking pricey, fragile items.

Next, the vacation spot should have a disability-friendly attitude or at the very least an awareness that people with disabilities are okay and that you don't have to pick up your toddler when one walks by. A good sign is a mechanism that allows people with disabilities to go to the front of the line, thus avoiding the long waits that many would be unable to tolerate.

Also, the vacation spot should have built-in places where the family can take some time off, out of direct sunshine, to cool down and relax. There should be lots of restrooms too. Family restrooms are best.

Consider which places suit the sensory proclivities of your child. Does your child love to spin around or bounce? Or is she fearful of movement or loud noise? Plan accordingly.

Our family has a lot of fun at theme parks, the seashore, and the outdoors. Danielle really loves vestibular stimulation, so any place where she can get spun around, bounced up and down, or swim works for her (and for us!). When we come back from such places, we all feel rested, refreshed, renewed, and strengthened.

You can too!

8
Developing a Prayer Life

For a parent of a child with autism, prayer is not an option. It is a necessity. The strength we need comes from our connectedness to sacred reality and from aligning ourselves with God, the source of all being. Prayer is the mechanism for doing this.

Jesus calls each one of us to prayer. A robust prayer life isn't reserved for those in the consecrated religious life. The Second Vatican Council emphasized this in the *Decree on the Laity*:

> Since Christ, sent by the Father, is the source and origin of the whole apostolate of the Church, the success of the lay apostolate depends upon the laity's living union with Christ, in keeping with the Lord's words, "He who abides in me, and I in him, bears much fruit, for without me you can do nothing" (John 15:5). This life of intimate union with Christ in the Church is nourished by spiritual aids which are common to all the faithful, especially active participation in the sacred liturgy. (5) These are to be used by the laity in such a way that while correctly fulfilling their secular duties in the ordinary conditions of life, they do not separate union with Christ from their life but rather performing their work according to God's will they grow in that union. In this way the laity must make progress in holiness in a happy and ready spirit, trying prudently and patiently to overcome difficulties.

We are called to a living union with Christ that is integrated into our ordinary lives. Many men and women are answering this call by embracing a deep spirituality and prayer life. I have seen the fruit of this, especially, in parishes that have men's and women's groups, which provide a way for people to explore their spirituality without feeling isolated. This is especially important for men, many of whom felt lampooned with the media's negative treatment of an emerging men's spirituality in the 1990s. However, men have started coming out of their lairs and are embracing a masculine spirituality again. Women went through much of this same soul-searching in the 70s and became comfortable with open spiritual interest. Both men and women need a robust prayer life. This is doubly true for a man or woman dealing with a special-needs child. So let us explore ways we can pray together.

What is prayer?

Prayer takes many forms. Yet all prayer is the turning of the mind and heart toward the sacred presence in our lives. As Catholic Christians we experience this presence as one God in three Persons, namely Father, Son, and Holy Spirit. The *Catechism of the Catholic Church* explains it in this way:

> Prayer is the life of the new heart. It ought to animate us at every moment. But we tend to forget him who is our life and our all. This is why the Fathers of the spiritual life in the Deuteronomic and prophetic traditions insist that prayer is a remembrance of God often awakened by the memory of the heart. "We must remember God more often than we draw breath." But we cannot pray "at all times" if we do not pray at specific times, consciously willing it. These are the special times of Christian prayer, both in intensity and duration.

Regardless of the particular type or technique, prayer is first and foremost a remembrance of God that tends to well up more from the emotional faculties, the heart, than from the mental faculties. There is a difference between prayer and theology. Moreover, prayer is life-giving and life-affirming. "It ought to animate us at every moment." Yet this spontaneous breaking in of God in our lives is something we cultivate and prepare for by conscious practice.

I like to think of prayer as a boat allowing us to cross over the waters that separate the mundane from the sacred. It is our vehicle of transformation, from seeing the world as something dead and mechanical to seeing it as something alive and spirit-filled. We have to do the hard work of rowing, but we are able to do this only because the water beneath the boat buoys us up. When I look at prayer this way, I am reminded of a haunting and beautiful Irish folk song called "The Water Is Wide."

> The water is wide, I cannot cross o'er,
> And neither have I wings to fly.
> Give me a boat that can carry two,
> And both shall row, my love and I.

All of us have the potential to develop a strong and authentic prayer life. We just have to begin. There are a wide variety of ways to pray depending on our individual temperament, circumstances, and faith history. We may pray in different ways at different times of our lives. But regardless of the type of prayer, God has given each of us the opportunity to draw near to him in a way that can transform and invigorate us. So let's take a look at some of the ways we can learn to respond to God's invitation to pray.

The Divine Office

The Divine Office (also Liturgy of the Hours) is a cycle of set prayers, primarily psalms, that are prayed at specific times of the day. Ordained priests and deacons are obligated to pray the Office, and laypeople are encouraged to pray it. Many parents of children with special needs find great insight and strength in this practice. Stuart Altshuler, whose eighteen-year-old son David has autism, told me how the Divine Office has become his primary form of prayer.

He said, "Once when I was praying to God for David to become more communicative and articulate his wants and needs to us, I got a really strong sense of God asking me, 'Stuart, how well are you articulating to me? How communicative are you to me?' I realized that we are all a bit communication impaired when it comes to communicating with the Lord, and I thought of St. John of the Cross and how my own dark night of the soul was a dryness in communicating with God."

Stuart told me that he realized how important listening was during prayer, and how the Divine Office is particularly suited to developing this faculty. "It forces you to articulate prayer but also to listen. In the Psalms one spends much of the time listening to God speaking through them. If you're having difficulty praying, I can think of no better prayer than the Divine Office."

Centering Prayer

Centering Prayer is a form of wordless self-emptying contemplative prayer where the practitioner figuratively falls through his false self and descends deeper and deeper into his true self until even this disappears and he is illumined by the Divine Presence only. It is an act of complete trust in God and openness to the action of God in our lives.

In 1989 I attended a workshop on Centering Prayer by Fr. Thomas Keating, a Trappist monk. He taught a technique whereby you choose a sacred word or phrase, usually a name of God or something associated with him. You sit quietly; as you breathe in and out, you imagine yourself descending into your true self. When thoughts or distractions intervene, you interiorly pronounce your sacred word and fall deeper and deeper into yourself. The word is a trigger for returning your mind and heart to God when they stray. During this practice I felt an increasing intimacy with God as the source and wellspring of all creation, including myself. Over time you experience the fiction of your false self and the reality of God and his creative force, from which all things flow. The effect was much like Insight Meditation but of a more overtly theistic nature. It was more like what is described by Meister Eckhart or the anonymous author of *The Cloud of Unknowing*.

This was years before Danielle was born. Little did I know at the time how important such a prayer practice would become to me as the father of a child with autism. Most of all I have learned that my thoughts and assumptions about life were not necessarily true just because I thought they were. In fact I've learned that my thoughts and assumptions were often plain wrong. God's reality is deeper and wider than our imaginings, and all we can do is trust him.

Christian yoga

Earlier I talked about the importance of parents having a set of daily practices to help them handle the stress of raising a family under very trying circumstances. Christian yoga can become such a daily practice.

Yoga means "to yoke" or "to join," as in an animal's yoke. In the days before mechanical engines, if you needed to prepare a field for planting, you would yoke a beast of burden to a plow. The yoke was a powerful tool for transformation: The earth could be broken, turned over, and made a suitable place for food to grow.

In a similar manner, yoga joins the mind, body, and spirit (breath) into a powerful tool of personal transformation. It integrates the parts of a person that we usually think of as separate. The yogi may yoke to postures, breathing, and conceptualizing. Once yoked, the range of body/mind movement is restricted and concentrated, and in such a state, awareness is heightened. Such acute awareness challenges the conceptual veil mistaken for absolute reality, with one result being that the yogi experiences life directly instead of merely thinking about life.

Yoga is usually associated with Hinduism and Buddhism, but it is a technique, not a religion. It is a practical method of experiencing one's own faith. Christian yoga uses postures, concentration, and breathing techniques in an overtly Christian context. An example of this would be performing a traditional yogic posture flow known as the Salute to the Sun while praying the Our Father. Also, Christian Yoga uses breath awareness as a relaxation device to still the mind and body as a preliminary step to imaginative and devotional practices. The ancient Jesus Prayer, practiced by the Desert Fathers, is an example of a traditional Christian practice that employs techniques very similar to yoga.

Practitioners of Christian yoga see in Jesus' teachings something quite like a yogic path. Certainly, the following saying from the Gospel according to Matthew is easy to read in a yogic context:

> Come to me, all you that are weary and are carrying
> heavy burdens, and I will give you rest. Take my yoke upon
> you, and learn from me; for I am gentle and humble in

heart, and you will find rest for your souls. For my yoke is easy, and my burden is light.

—Matthew 11:28–30

Parents of children with autism and other serious disabilities desperately want to respond to this invitation to find rest. We feel overburdened and overworked. We feel stressed out and in need of spiritual rest. We long to yoke ourselves to the path on which Jesus calls us to follow him. Christian yoga sees the path of Jesus as one that carries us away from everything that keeps us from the kingdom of God. It is a way to cultivate a means of self-healing and forgiveness by increasing our receptivity to grace.

I was a Christian yoga instructor in my younger years, so it should come as no surprise that I am a big fan of this approach. I encourage parents of children with special needs to explore Christian yoga in greater detail. A good place to start would be with the works of Jesuit Anthony de Mello and Benedictine J. M. Dechanet.

The Spiritual Exercises of St. Ignatius Loyola

Many people have found the *Spiritual Exercises* of St. Ignatius Loyola to be highly beneficial as they seek to discern God's will in their lives and then live it fully. It is undertaken over four weeks on retreat, or it can be done over a longer period of time privately at home. Usually, the exercises are performed under the guidance of a spiritual director.

The *Exercises* use visualization and imaginative prayer to develop a connection with Jesus and an awareness of God's great love for us. Anyone interested in learning more about the *Spiritual Exercises* can find a wealth of information at the website IgnatianSpirituality.com.

The Rosary

Many parents of children with special needs derive great spiritual benefit from the rosary. Tradition tells us that the rosary was given to St. Dominic by the Blessed Mother herself, and the practice is closely associated with devotion to Mary. The rosary can be prayed privately or in group settings, such as prayer services and other gatherings.

The rosary is prayed with a set of beads grouped into "decades," while meditating on a series of sacred mysteries in the life of Jesus and his mother, Mary. The individual beads are reminders to pray one of three main prayers: the Our Father, the Hail Mary, or the Glory Be. The rosary begins with a recitation of the Apostle's Creed and ends with the Hail, Holy Queen. It can be an intense spiritual experience that leads the practitioner to a deep awareness of God's mercy and holiness.

Praise is an important element in each of the prayers that make up the rosary. Over time I have learned the value of praise. It not only lifts up our hearts and minds to God but also allows us to express the joy and happiness we feel as children of God. This is therapeutic and restorative, especially when we are struggling to learn how best to embrace the life God has given us as mother or father of a child with a serious disability.

Prayers of intercession

Prayers of intercession are prayer requests to God either directly or through a saint. This is what most people think of when they hear the word *prayer*. Jesus taught his followers that they should ask for what they need. He said that just as humans know how to give good things to our children, so, too, does God desire to help each of us. A good portion of the Our Father is intercessory prayer: "Give us this day our daily bread. . . . Forgive us our trespasses. . . . Deliver us from evil." In the Gospels, Jesus is asked by many people to heal them or their loved ones. He taught that with sufficient faith you could ask for a mountain to fall into the sea and it would be done.

Many of us rely on prayers of intercession to generate the confidence we need to get through life, especially when faced with difficulty. Asking God for what we want and need helps us to see clearly and to move toward these things confidently. When we are raising a child with a serious disability, we turn to God for help frequently. We need to know that God is there to help us on our difficult path. With this confidence we are able to live our lives in sincerity and truth.

Prayers of intercession give voice to our hopes and expectations. One of the most notable effects I've experienced from asking God for help is a reduction in anxiety. When we give our needs to God, we are relieved of the fear that we must shoulder the burden ourselves. The effect of this can be very calming.

This sentiment was expressed by Kathleen from Ohio. During her son Connor's brain surgery she was too nervous to say prayers, but she found her mind silently repeating, *Sacred Heart of Jesus, I place my trust in thee* over and over. This gave her the peace of mind to get through the ordeal.

In the Catholic tradition, intercessory prayers sometimes take the form of a novena, a series of prayers over nine days that is usually directed to a saint. Traditionally, certain saints are associated with particular types of intercessions. An example is St. Jude, patron of hopeless cases.

My wife, Mercedes, sometimes turns to St. Gerard Majella for help. He is a saint often invoked by women wishing to become pregnant, have a safe labor and delivery, and endure any other difficulty that comes with being a mother. It makes sense that the mother of a child with special needs would find strength in this saint. Mothers of children with disabilities often find strength in saints who themselves were mothers. One of them was St. Monica, who endured many trials on account of her wayward son St. Augustine. And, of course, there is the Blessed Virgin Mary, who saw her own Son die on the cross. Fathers may find it comforting to pray to St. Joseph, the patriarch Abraham, or even Adam, the prototypical man and father.

Likewise, it is nice to know that friends and relatives are keeping you in their prayers. On my desk is a card from Medjugorje dated August 2004 and informing us in several languages that Mass would be said on Danielle's behalf. It was sent to us by cousins Bernard and Jeanette while on pilgrimage there. Countless relatives and friends have remembered Danielle in their prayers, and we are grateful for their efforts. In the same way Kathleen told me that on the day before Connor's surgery his cousins arranged for a healing Mass in his honor. "It was very comforting and peaceful, and emotional. So many people praying for Connor. I could feel the love, and it made me feel good."

Teaching prayer to our special-needs children

Children with significant developmental disabilities can be taught how to pray. Repetition is very helpful. The more you can build prayer into your family's life, the better it will "take" with your children. An example is saying grace at meals. Its ritualistic featuresuntil, including the sign of the cross, followed by the traditional "Bless us, O Lord," make learning this prayer easy through practice. The powerful natural reinforcement of getting to eat afterward helps too. Before you know it, your special-needs child, if verbal, will be saying the words along with you. If nonverbal, he or she will at the very least attempt the mechanics of crossing himself and waiting until the prayer is finished before eating.

The sign of the cross can actually be very difficult, even for typical children (and some adults). Children with autism can have trouble imitating gestures and may need hand-over-hand assistance or a sequencing device to master it. Our *Adaptive First Eucharist Preparation Kit* contains a puzzle activity to teach the sequence.

Lately, I have taken to putting short prayers on Danielle's electronic speech device. This machine has a display of picture icons, which the nonverbal child selects. The machine turns this into spoken words for all to hear. So now at meals, when it is time for grace, Danielle pushes a button on the machine and "says" grace with the rest of us. For longer prayers such as the Hail Mary or Our Father, it is best to break the prayer up into shorter phrases, which are easier for the nonverbal child to understand. The device even allows you to make up your own prayers, such as "Jesus, I love you!" and "Thank you God!" At bedtime try "Dear God, thank you for this day." The main thing is to build prayer into your everyday activities so that it becomes natural in the mind of the child to acknowledge God at appropriate moments to mark the rhythm and flow of life.

One of the most beloved Catholic prayers is the rosary. Darlene and Stuart Altschuler have developed a creative way to teach the rosary to the children in their sacramental preparation program for children with special needs. They found that rosary beads were a bit too stimulating for most of the kids, who would twirl them or try to wear the beads as a necklace. So they developed a rosary poster and talk board. The poster is a big visual representation of the rosary with Velcro for each "bead." The class prays the rosary together in the following manner. One child comes up to the talk board and selects a prayer icon representing the Hail Mary, Our Father, or Glory Be and attaches this to the "bead" on the rosary poster. One by one each child does the same until the decade is complete. The decade ends with the appropriate mystery, presented with a highly visual poster.

Darlene says that the children approach this version of the rosary with deep reverence. "It is remarkable, the spirituality that has come out of this practice, the reverence," she says. "I can't even describe it."

A Family Activity
The Rosary Garden

There is a Cistercian monastery just a couple of miles from my home in New Jersey. It is a lovely place, with expansive fields, a church, various monastic buildings, and a beautiful rosary garden. Every once in a while my wife and I take the kids, and we stroll among the life-size statues that depict the mysteries of the rosary. It is a nice way to spend a summer evening and expose the kids to the serenity one finds in such places.

On this particular evening Mercedes and I were accompanied by Danielle and Shannon. The first thing we saw upon our arrival was a family of wild turkeys, including a tom, several hens, and many chicks, pecking for food in the meadow adjoining the parking lot. We headed toward the church as there was a prayer service going on, and we stepped inside. It was a healing service, which Mercedes and I both needed.

After the service we walked to the rosary garden. It is a trail that winds around a small lake with large stone statues, free-standing and relief, each showing one of the fifteen mysteries. There are benches where you can sit and pray a decade at a time in front of the appropriate statue. However, this evening we simply walked through the garden and admired the statues. I explained to Shannon and to Danielle what each one meant. Both girls enjoyed putting themselves into the scenes among the statues, while Mercedes and I remarked on the prayerfulness we felt there.

When we were leaving this beautiful place, Shannon caught sight of something out of the car window. There were at least a dozen deer grazing in the soybean field at twilight. I felt as though we were surrounded by beauty wherever we went.

9
Miracles, Meaning, and Healing

All human beings share a need for healing. If you live long enough, you will find occasions when life is hard and painful. This is a cornerstone of our shared humanity. Christians see this need for healing dramatically portrayed and fulfilled in the life, death, and Resurrection of Jesus Christ. It's important that we acknowledge our common woundedness. Otherwise, we run the risk of seeing our own private suffering as the only valid suffering, the only suffering sanctified by God. Such thinking separates us from others and leaves us feeling stuck and isolated.

However, I do think we parents of children with disabilities can see our own specific predicament as the path toward healing that God has laid out for us. We can negotiate this path successfully by learning how to forge meaning out of what has seemed a cruel joke. When we discover that there is an answer to the question of why this has happened, healing becomes possible. Usually we discover this answer in some kind of an intuitive fashion. Bernice, the mother of twins, told me, "You always question, I think, why God has allowed it to happen to you, especially with twins—one very bright and intelligent, while the other has significant challenges." It was important for Bernice to discover why Donald had so many challenges while his sister Desiree was a stand-out student. I have found this quest for meaning to be a very common theme in the healing of parents of children with special needs.

Maria Rioux, whose eldest son, Thomas, has Down syndrome, put it to me rather succinctly when she said, "God gives us these children for a reason, not because he's having a moment."

How our children affect others

Part of the meaning is found in the way children with disabilities can be catalysts for change in the lives of those who come into contact with them. They force us to love beyond our previous ability to love. Sherry Boas, whose adopted daughter Teresa has Down syndrome, said, "Having a child with a disability brings about an unselfishness that is crucial for spiritual growth."

Sherry's desire for meaning lay at the center of her decision to adopt Teresa. She and her husband, Phil, did not originally intend to adopt a child with Down syndrome but "wanted to be open to whatever God had in store." One day, they received a call from Catholic Social Services asking them if they would consider adopting a child with Down syndrome. They struggled and prayed over the decision. They learned that many children with Down syndrome are aborted, and they began to see significant meaning in this opportunity to be open to life. When Phil said to Sherry, "We might as well make this all mean something," they both decided they would adopt five-week-old Teresa. Sherry spoke eloquently to me about the gift that people with Down syndrome have to offer us. Sherry has written a series of novels called The Lily Trilogy, centering on how a young woman with Down syndrome affects her family in a wide variety of ways.

I was particularly touched when Sherry told me of an epiphany she had experienced with her adopted daughter Teresa.

"It was during a rosary after Mass when I noticed that Teresa was down on her knees with her hands folded in prayer. We were just sitting. She had done the rosary far more prayerfully than we had. Seeing this I said to myself, *So this is why God sent me Teresa.*

I began to see her as a gift, and realized the sacrifices involved in raising a child with a disability could be a route to holiness."

Sometimes parents experience a healing when we experience how our children can become a transformative force in the lives of others, even total strangers. Mercedes and I have experienced this on many occasions. We are not unique. Darlene Altschuler, who runs the special-needs sacramental preparation program I described earlier, describes one example. At special Masses for the program, parents and their children with special needs sit together in a reserved seating area in the church. This provides structure for children who benefit from it, and it's a practical arrangement in a 125-year-old church built long before anyone thought about handicapped accessibility. At one of these special Masses Darlene noticed a woman from the parish crying as she sat near the children in reserved seats. After Mass the woman came up to Darlene and with tears in her eyes said, "Thank you so much for letting me sit with your group today." Evidently this woman had found healing in the company of this group of children with disabilities. Darlene told me that this sort of thing happens regularly. "People write notes saying how glad they are to be present at our special Masses."

Our disabled God

"We worship a disabled God," said Sister Bonnie passionately. We had been talking about the way our children can have such a healing effect on others. She meant that the twisted, distorted, and disfigured image of Jesus on the cross shows how God allowed himself to become completely disabled and at the same time completely accessible to human beings in need of healing. Because we can see the image and likeness of God in the disabled Jesus, we can also see the image and likeness of God in the child or adult with a disability. This recognition moves us toward compassion and heals us of our own afflictions because it is such a concrete manifestation of God's great love for us and his saving power.

I told Sister Bonnie that I was reminded of Father Richard Rohr's notion of "liminal space," that in-between sacred space where transformation happens. I was thinking about how Jesus hanging on the cross suspended between heaven and earth was our point of intersection with God, and that this disabled figure reminded me of a painting by Salvador Dali entitled *The Christ of St. John of the Cross.*

Sister Bonnie reached for a postcard on her desk and handed it to me saying, "Is this what you mean?" I was stunned. It was a postcard of that very painting. Dali shows Jesus hung on the cross above the earth, viewed from behind with his head dropped below his shoulders in a steep angle looking downward. Both Sister Bonnie and I were independently grappling with the same question and in the same way. I saw how our children were indeed images of our disabled God and began to understand how they could awaken compassion in others and become a focus for our own healing.

Seeing miracles

One of the best things about being the parent of a child with special needs is learning how to see the very real miracles that happen in everyday life.

These miracles are the everyday accomplishments that so many of us might take for granted, such as learning to speak or to use a picture system, electronic device, or sign language. These can seem miraculous to the parent of a child with disabilities. I remember the day when Danielle learned to call me "Dad" on her electronic speech device. She was almost thirteen and had never called me Dad before. That was a miracle! When you are the mother or father of a child with a serious disability, you look through a different lens. When your child learns to button a coat, write his name, or cooperate for a routine dental cleaning, you realize that there truly is a God and he was there today for you and your child. At such times I have been caught breaking into an off pitch rendition of the song "I Could Not Ask for More" by Diane Warren.

> These are the moments
> I know heaven must exist.
> These are the moments
> I know all I need is this.

For parents of kids with disabilities, the workings of medical science can cause us to marvel and thank God the way supernatural miracles do. Kathleen and Bob never stopped praying for this kind of a "miracle" for their son Connor. You will recall that he suffered from a very rare medical condition called hypothalamic hamartoma, a nonmalignant tumor on the hypothalamus of the brain that causes severe seizures on a daily basis.

"I was praying more than I ever prayed in my life, but there were no answers from the doctors or from God," said Kathleen. "Then we heard of a doctor from Australia who was pioneering an experimental deep brain surgery on children like Connor."

She explained that her family even contemplated traveling to Australia, but as luck would have it, the doctor planned on coming to the United States to look for kids with Connor's condition who were good candidates for the surgery. Kathleen, Bob, Connor, and Christopher went to Phoenix, and the doctor agreed to do the surgery on Connor. "The surgery was a big success. Connor no longer has seizures. Since then he has made great improvements in all areas. He still is delayed in many respects and has some residual problems, but it's nothing like it was before the surgery. It was a true miracle!" exclaimed Kathleen.

Although Connor's story may seem exceptional, it does point to the truth that such healings do happen sometimes. While acceptance of the reality of the disability is a necessary step in our own healing process, it doesn't mean that we shouldn't continue to ask God to intervene. We should not presume to limit God's freedom here. But we do well to remember that the most important healing is healing of the spirit. Conversion, change of heart, acceptance of the child's disabilities, acts of generosity—those are the types of healings we are more likely to experience.

Certainly the Jesus we encounter in the Gospels is in many respects a miracle worker and healer. But the most consistent message he gives to the people who approach him looking for healing is that their faith has already healed them. In a very real way, Jesus gives us leave of everything that ails us, everything that keeps us from the kingdom of God. The ordinary and the extraordinary miracles of life lead me to marvel at the inherent goodness of God and the full breadth of his saving power.

I like to think that such miracles come wrapped in praise. There is something about praise that brings about spiritual growth. I've found that praise is most powerful when it grows out of our trials and rises from the ashes of the life we have come to embrace. Praise from someone who has never suffered can sound hollow, but when someone who has suffered loss is able to praise, this authentic singing resonates deep within us on a visceral level.

You and I have endured the pain of learning our children have serious disabilities. We have endured the loss of the child we imagined we would have, and learned to find joy in the changeling child God has gifted each of us with. When we rediscover our ability to praise, that is when magic happens.

The poet Rainer Maria Rilke once wrote,

To praise is the whole thing! A man who can praise
comes toward us like ore out of the silences
of rock. His heart, that dies, presses out
for others a wine that is fresh forever.

Praising is a powerful experience for the special-needs community. For the past five years Sister Bonnie has been visiting adults
with disabilities in group homes to provide an opportunity for
the residents to praise, pray, and sing together. "It can get very
charismatic." I have seen such outpourings of the Spirit in my
interactions with adults who have developmental and cognitive
disabilities too. It is a spontaneous and joyous experience of God
in our midst.

Moving beyond the blame game

One thing I've learned is that people love to find someone they
can blame for their troubles. Though this may be a natural first
response during a crisis, it's not a useful strategy in the long run.
Failure to move beyond the blame game can end up leaving us
feeling depressed, exhausted, and disheartened. Most often we
blame God and ourselves.

It's okay to bounce off the ropes, dazed and semiconscious
from the beating you just received when you realized your son or
daughter had autism or some other serious disability, and blame
either God or yourself for the knockout punch. So stop feeling
guilty about that. As I said, it's a natural *first* response. Before we
can move beyond it, though, we need to move *through* it. But the
secret is not to stay stuck there, holding on so tightly to our need
to blame that we forget how to loosen our fingers and allow the
blame to subside and then pass.

The tendency to blame God isn't always just a first reaction
to shocking news. It can linger. People get angry at God and stay

angry. It really is hard to understand why bad things happen in a world created by a loving God. There's no satisfying intellectual answer to it. The answer is spiritual. When it comes, it's is one of the miracles I talked about above. When it comes, we know that Jesus stands with us in our trials, that God knows exactly what we're going through.

Self-blame can linger too. Although today we no longer ascribe illness and mental disorders to demonic possession or the sins of the parents, the modern equivalents of this could be genetics, exposure to environmental toxins, and other causes. We can and often do feel blameworthy about these things. Genetics, especially, can be a source of self-blame because it can be distorted in our minds to awaken some deep and secret flaw in ourselves that we were supposed to know about before being so foolish as to have children. As I said, this view is very distorted. Still other examples of self-blame might include sentiments such as "If only I hadn't had my child vaccinated" or "I should have known better than to put down so many lawn chemicals." You can drive yourself crazy in the blame game.

These kinds of guilt trips are destructive, and we need to recognize them for what they are and move beyond them. The same is true about any anger we may feel about God's role in all this.

Because the truth of the matter is that God loves us more than we can possibly know. It is our faith in the reality of God's love that can allow us to move through our initial anger and sorrow, and find whatever underlying meaning exists.

We need to know how much we are loved. I remember being on retreat many years ago and hearing a story from a man who lived in an orphanage as a boy. He would stand by the ocean and hope that at least the ocean loved him. I wish I knew this man's name, because his story made a deep impression on me. I thought about this and visualized a scene where the ocean answers the boy by unequivocally proclaiming a depth of love beyond anything the boy had imagined. I have returned to this scene time and time again and felt a kinship with the boy who just needed to know that something as big as the ocean loved him. Parents of children with serious disabilities need to know the depth of God's love for them too and rejoice in it. Likewise, parents can be such an ocean to their own children.

A Family Activity
Cultivate an Attitude of Praise

Instead of being caught in the blame game, why not cultivate an attitude of praise? It is something you can do in secret that will facilitate healing in yourself and in your family. It doesn't cost you anything, and it's easy to learn.

Here's what you do. Visualize yourself telling everyone in the family three things you particularly like about them. Start with your spouse. These compliments must be real; no damning with faint praise. When you have finished, find three things you consider praiseworthy about yourself. Don't make a negative comment or criticize or find fault. Do this every day.

This may be hard at first, since we are so used to finding fault, especially in ourselves. But this is not an examination of conscience. It is meant to restore balance to our habitually negative self-talk. It is meant to generate positive, healing, sentiments and affirmations. This activity should be life-affirming, not life-denying. It is a way to teach us to think about ourselves and others in as positive a way as God thinks about us.

By cultivating an attitude of praise, we begin to feel lighter and better about ourselves. We stop seeing everything and everyone in such negative terms. Hope returns, and we begin to notice how old wounds are being healed. We feel energized again and ripe for physical and spiritual transformation.

10
Concluding Remarks

One thing I've learned from being on this path is that there are both ups and downs. In the blink of an eye old behaviors can reemerge, and new problems surface like a submarine that has just crossed under the polar ice cap. But if you ride it out and put things in perspective, things quiet down again. You really come to appreciate your life and all its rhythms and rests. Most of all you come to appreciate everyone in your family and the gift each one is to you. You come to appreciate God as the giver of such precious gifts. When we realize that suffering comes to everyone, that it is woven into the fabric of life, that we can see it modeled in Jesus' Passion, death and resurrection, then we can see how parents of children with severe disabilities (and everyone else) are being invited to walk this mysterious path with Jesus.

Humor is important

There is much humor in raising a child with special needs. If I can leave just one piece of advice to parents, it would be this: allow yourselves to laugh again. A while after Danielle had been diagnosed, I realized that I had stopped laughing. This was a revelation and led me to rediscover the humor in my life.

An example is the day I received a frantic call from Mercedes telling me that Danielle had pulled over the fish tank and spilled our two goldfish onto the floor. Mercedes was upset because she could find only one of the fish. The other was missing and presumed dead. Several hours later I got home and searched for the missing fish. I found it, apparently lifeless, lodged behind a piece of furniture. Colin wanted to give his fish a proper burial, so we took it outside to our backyard, which was covered in snow. I dug a small hole in the frozen ground and placed the fish in this shallow grave. But before I could cover it up Colin called out, "Wait. He's moving! He's still alive!" I filled a bowl with water and put the goldfish in. To my astonishment, the fish started to swim like a sailboat listing heavily to one side. An hour later it was swimming normally, so I placed it back in the fish tank. We renamed it Lazarus because it had been raised from the dead, so to speak. Do you know that Lazarus went on to live for two more years with no apparent deficits! I still laugh when I think about it.

Often parents of special-needs kids will appreciate the unique humor when others can't. Thomas, a young man with Down syndrome, started to receive Holy Communion under both species, bread and wine. Maria his mother noticed that he would drink a lot of wine—more than most would consider appropriate. When she asked him why he drank so much wine, Thomas explained that the more wine he took the more grace he would receive from the sacrament. Maria recognized the humor in this although almost no one else in the parish thought it was funny. She explained, "Kansas is still at heart a dry state, so some people might be just a bit more sensitive on this subject than others."

One more story. One evening we were entertaining a family of guests from Arizona at our home. It got late, and Danielle asked to go to bed, using both her communication device and sign language. However, we were enjoying the company and the conversation, so we told Danielle to wait and just sit on the couch a while longer. We kept talking, and Danielle got sleepier. Finally, she scanned the pages of her communication device feverishly, then touched some icons, and the machine announced, "All done, time to go home!" We all laughed (and Danielle got to go to bed).

It's nice when the humor of the moment overtakes you and you find yourself laughing spontaneously. Laughter is therapeutic too. Some say that laughter is associated with stronger immune systems, a lower rate of cancer, and less stress. I can believe it. I had lost laughter for a time. Thanks to the abundant graces of our God, I have been able to find laughter again.

Embrace it!

It's important to embrace the life we have with our children. Humor is just one way for us to embrace it. The way we view our life, how we think and talk about it, and how we act in response to the circumstances in which we find ourselves makes an enormous difference. If our attitude is positive and accepting, we are better able to deal with the very real challenges we encounter. Embrace this life—even when we are like Jacob wrestling the angel at Hebron. Embrace this life—even when sorrow from deep within us wells up into tears.

This does not mean that we don't pray for things to be better. Rather it means that we accept responsibility for our own happiness or unhappiness, for our own relationship to a loving God and Father, or for the distance that lies between us and still needs to be bridged. Isn't this what free will is about? God is giving us an opportunity to respond with an enthusiastic yes! Jesus tells us, "I came that they have life, and have it abundantly."

When we live this way, then each moment, each breath, becomes an opportunity to deepen our own spirituality. This is particularly true when we are able to encounter the spiritual domain in the way our children do—in visual, intuitive, and imagistic silence. I've mentioned how I gained a deeper appreciation of the sacraments and of God when I allowed myself to interpret reality this way. I've also gained a better appreciation and understanding of my daughter's spiritual potential. In a sense, she became my spiritual advisor. I learned as much from her as she learned from me.

Likewise, parenting a child with a severe disability can become an opportunity to deepen our marriage. There's a rumor out there that parents of special-needs children have a 90 percent divorce rate; in fact, they are less likely to divorce than parents of typical children. There's a reason for this. Just think about how much these parents have to do as a united couple just to provide a decent, dignified life for their special-needs child. They have to advocate together, problem solve, resolve child-care issues, battle school boards, and support each other through very trying circumstances. Mercedes and I have come to depend on each another much more than we would if we did not have a child with autism.

The Catholic church sees sacramental marriage as a sign of the unconditional and all-encompassing love that God has for each of us. The sacramental character of marriage is both tested and strengthened by the experience.

Last, the experience of being a special-needs parent provides us an opportunity to deepen our commitment to community and the church. In our compassionate response to the needs of our own children, we discover that there is an entire community of vulnerable people out there in need of the help we can give them. When we move beyond our own personal and private isolation, we discover the community we so desperately need. In the same way, the church is given the opportunity to accept its role of providing spiritual comfort and community to people with disabilities and their families by welcoming us and administering the sacraments to us.

Over the rainbow

Being the parent of a child with autism or another disability is a lot like the movie *The Wizard of Oz*. The film starts in black and white on the Kansas prairie. Dorothy is a young girl who dreams of what lies on the other end of the rainbow. A tornado transports her to the colorful and adventurous Land of Oz, where she finds herself caught up in a great adventure. However, she longs to be home with her family in Kansas again. To her astonishment she learns that she had the ability to return there anytime by clicking her heels three times and repeating "There's no place like home." It's easy for us to long for an escape to Oz. It may even be desirable for a short time, but hopefully we discover, as Dorothy did, that you can't run away from your problems; you have to face them with the people you love.

We who put our faith in God trust that he has created us all for a purpose. That purpose is to experience the love that freely flows out of his creative power. If we believe that God is the source and author of all, and we are made in his image and likeness, then we know with confidence that we are all spiritually enabled. We must find meaning in the sacred places where we are standing.

I think that we discover these sacred places in our everyday lives. Earlier I drew a parallel between the obstacles we encounter as parents of children with severe disabilities and the holy mountains where God is said to dwell. You don't find God in easy places. You find God in rugged, windswept places. You find God in the places you were too scared to go until you woke up one morning and found yourself on the summit.

In closing, I'd like to reflect on the words of Zechariah, the father of St. John the Baptist. After his son was born, Zechariah prophesied that John would play a major role in salvation history by heralding the public ministry of Jesus. As parents of children with disabilities, each one of us can see ourselves in the manner of Zechariah, standing over our own child with hands raised in a blessing as we repeat these words:

> And you, child, will be called the prophet of the Most
>   High;
>   for you will go before the Lord to prepare his ways,
> to give knowledge of salvation to his people
>   by the forgiveness of their sins.
> By the tender mercy of our God,
>   the dawn from on high will break upon us,
> to give light to those who sit in darkness and in the shadow
>   of death,
>   to guide our feet into the way of peace.
>
> —Luke 1:76–79

Resources

Sacramental Preparation

David and Mercedes Rizzo, *Adaptive First Eucharist Preparation Kit for Children with Autism and Other Special Needs* (Chicago: Loyola Press, 2012). www.loyolapress.com

United States Conference of Catholic Bishops, Inc., *Guidelines for the Celebration of the Sacraments with Persons with Disabilities* (Washington, DC, 1995).

Support Groups

Autism Society
4340 East-West Highway
Suite 350
Bethesda, MD 20814
Tel. 800-328-8476
www.autism-society.org

United Cerebral Palsy (UCP)
1825 K Street NW
Suite 600
Washington, DC 20006
800-872-5827
www.ucp.org

National Association for Down Syndrome (NADS)
Box 206
Wilmette, IL 60091
630-325-9112
www.nads.org

National Down Syndrome Congress (NDSC)
30 Mansell Court
Suite 108
Rosewell, GA 30076
800-232-NDSC (6372)
www.ndsccenter.org

National Down Syndrome Society (NDSS)
666 Broadway, 8th Floor
New York, NY 10012
800-221-4602
www.ndss.org

Hypothalamic Hamartoma Uncontrolled Gelastic Seizures
(HHUGS)
www.hhugs.com

Links to Parent Support Groups for Children with Motor
Impairment: www.childrensdisabilities.info/cerebral_palsy/
groups-motorimpairment.html

Foundations and Organizations

Epilepsy Foundation
8301 Professional Place
Landover, MD 20785
800-332-1000
www.epilepsyfoundation.org

Best Day Foundation
567 Auto Center Drive
Suite 6
Watsonville, CA 95076
800-309-2815
www.bestdayfoundation.org

National Catholic Partnership on Disability (NCPD)
415 Michigan Avenue NE
Suite 95
Washington, DC 20017-4501
202-529-2933
www.ncpd.org

Vanderbilt Kennedy Center
Vanderbilt University
PMB 40
230 Appleton Place
Nashville, TN 37203-5721
615-322-8240
www.kc.vanderbilt.edu

L'Arche USA
1130 SW Morrison Street
Suite 230
Portland, OR 97205
503-282-6231
www.larcheusa.org

Links to Disability, Religion and Spirituality Resources from
Vanderbilt Kennedy Center
kc.vanderbilt.edu/Kennedy_pdfs/spirituality/
DisabilityReligionSpiritualityResources1108.pdf

Families and Children with Special Needs

Cindy N. Ariel and Robert A. Naseef, eds., *Voices from the Spectrum: Parents, Grandparents, Siblings, People with Autism, and Professionals Share Their Wisdom* (London, UK, and Philadelphia, PA: Jessica Kingsley Publishers, 2006).

Robert A. Naseef, *Special Children, Challenged Parents: The Struggles and Rewards of Raising a Child with a Disability* (Baltimore, MD: Paul H. Brookes Publishing Co., 2001).

Spirituality and Prayer

Henri Nouwen Society
P. O. Box 250522,
343 S. Kirkwood Road, Suite 5,
St. Louis, MO 63122
866-226-2158
www.henrinouwen.org

Centering Prayer www.centeringprayer.com

Contemplative Outreach, Ltd.
10 Park Place
2nd Floor, Suite B
Butler, NJ 07405
973-838-3384
www.contemplativeoutreach.org
Information on Centering Prayer, the lectio divina, and welcoming prayer

Divine Office
divineoffice.org
An online guide to the Divine Office

Christian Yoga
www.christianyoga.us

DeMello Spirituality Center
Fordham University
Faber Hall
Bronx, New York 10458
718-817-4508
www.demello.org

J. M. Dechanet OSB, *Yoga in Ten Lessons.*
A classic introduction to Christian yoga by one of its early advocates. Although this is out of print, it can still be found at libraries, in used book stores, and through Internet vendors.

Ignatian Spirituality
http://ignatianspirituality.com

Thomas Merton Center and The International
Thomas Merton Society
Bellarmine University
2001 Newburg Road
Louisville, Kentucky 40205
www.merton.org

Center for Action and Contemplation
PO Box 12464
Albuquerque, NM 87195
505-242-9588
www.cacradicalgrace.org/richard-rohr

Insight Meditation Society
1230 Pleasant Street
Barre, MA 01005
Tel. 978-355-4378
www.dharma.org
An excellent resource for information on the Buddhist practice
of Insight Meditation

References

Chapter 1

"The individual's whole experience is built upon the plan of his language" is from Henri Delacroix, *Les Grandes Formes de la Vie Mentale*.

Albert Einstein on nonverbal thinking quoted in Jacques Hadamard, *The Psychology of Invention in the Mathematical Field* (Princeton, NJ: Princeton University Press, 1945, 1973), 142.

Poetry from St. John of the Cross, "The Dark Night," translated by Robert Bly, read by Bly on a YouTube video: http://www.youtube.com/watch?v=PbsgD3m3MY4.

Chapter 2

"All that I have written seems like straw to me." Thomas Aquinas, quoted in Brian Davies, *The Thought of Thomas Aquinas* (New York: Oxford University Press, 1993), 9.

The story of St. Augustine and the boy at the beach is recounted in Jacobus de Voragine, *The Golden Legend: Readings on the Saints*, vol. 2, William Granger Ryan, trans. (Princeton, NJ: Princeton University Press, 1993), 116.

"Mercy within mercy within mercy" from Thomas Merton, *The Sign of Jonas* (Orlando, FL: Harcourt, 1953), 362.

Richard Rohr on "being serious about the questions" is adapted from his audiotape "Holding the Tension: The Power of Paradox" and published on the Web site www.emergingchristian.com/category/richard-rohr.

Chapter 4

The discussion of clowns was derived from an article by Lori M. Culwell entitled "The Role of the Clown in Shakespeare's Theatre," published at http://extra.shu.ac.uk/emls/iemls/shaksper/files/ROLE%20CLOWN.txt.

"Silence is the only Voice of our God," from Herman Melville, *Pierre: or, The Ambiguities* (New York: Penguin Books, 1996), 204.

"O sleepless as the river under thee . ..," from Hart Crane, "To Brooklyn Bridge" in *The Bridge: A Poem by Hart Crane* (New York: Liveright Publishing Corporation, 1970), 2.

Chapter 5

The U.S. Catholic Bishops on Penance and Reconciliation from *Guidelines for the Celebration of the Sacraments with Persons with Disabilities* (Washington, DC: United States Conference of Catholic Bishops, Inc., 1995), paragraph 23.

Early Christian celebration of the Eucharist from *The Didache: The Lord's Teaching Through the Twelve Apostles to the Nations*, Roberts-Donaldson English Translation, published at www.earlychristianwritings.com/text/didache-roberts.html.

"Eucharistic Prayer II" from *The Roman Missal*, © 2010, International Commission on English in the Liturgy.

The U.S. Catholic Bishops on the liturgy being accessible to persons with disabilities from *Pastoral Statement of U.S. Catholic Bishops on Persons with Disabilities,* November 1978; revised 1989, *in Guidelines for the Celebration of the Sacraments with Persons with Disabilities* (Washington, DC: United States Conference of Catholic Bishops, Inc., Washington, DC, 1995), 1.

The bishops on the Eucharist from *Guidelines for the Celebration of the Sacraments with Persons with Disabilities*, paragraph 20. On Confirmation, paragraph 16. On matrimonial consent, paragraph 37.

"That is no country for old men. . . ." William Butler Yeats, "Sailing to Byzantium" in *The Norton Anthology of Poetry: Revised Shorter Edition* (New York: W. W. Norton & Company, 1975), 444.

Chapter 6

The Catechism on the dignity of the human person from *Catechism of the Catholic Church Second Edition* (Washington, DC: United States Catholic Conference, 1994, 1997), paragraph 1700.

Henri Nouwen on the great paradox of ministry from Henri Nouwen, *Gracias! A Latin American Journal* (New York: Harper & Row, 1983), 19.

Chapter 7

"The universe is unfolding as it should. . . ." from Max Ehrmann, "Desiderata," 1926.

The legend of Thor and Midgard from Donald A. Mackenzie, *Teutonic Myth and Legend* (London: Gresham Publishing Company, 1912), 104.

Chapter 8

The Catechism on prayer, *Catechism of the Catholic Church,* paragraph 2697.

Chapter 9

"To praise is the whole thing! . . ." Rainer Maria Rilke, Sonnet VII in *Selected Poems of Rainer Maria Rilke*, Robert Bly, trans. (New York: Harper & Row, 1981).

Also Available

Adaptive First Eucharist Preparation Kit
For Individuals with Autism and Other Special Needs

3580-1
1 kit: $59.95 each
2–5 kits: $49.99 each
6–10 kits: $39.99 each

The learning tools in this kit are based on tested, proven strategies that have been used successfully by people with autism and other special needs to fully experience their faith and become prepared to receive the Eucharist.

To order, call 800-621-1008
or visit www.loyolapress.com/special-needs

Growing Your Faith Community

Whether you're searching the Web, using social media, or reading text on your mobile device, Loyola Press supports your catechetical mission with meaningful and inspiring content based on sound doctrine.

Share knowledge, mentor peers, and grow in faith with other parish leaders at *DRE Connect*.

dreconnect.loyolapress.com

Access practical advice and discussions hosted by Joe Paprocki, DMin, on *Catechist's Journey*. View webinars, ask questions, and download free resources.

catechistsjourney.loyolapress.com

Connect with us on the following:

Facebook
facebook.com/loyolapress

Twitter
twitter.com/loyolapress

You Tube
youtube.com/loyolapress